Rebecca Lister is an award-winning playwright, arts producer and social worker. She is the co-artistic director of arts company Anvil Productions and the education manager of Eating Disorders Victoria. She was born and raised in Mount Isa but has lived in many places in Australia. In 2018 she was awarded the Australia Day Mount Isa City Council 'Spirit of Mount Isa' Award.

Tony Kelly is a native title lawyer and is currently CEO of First Nations Legal and Research Services in Melbourne. He previously worked as a social worker specialising in at-risk young people and as a park ranger in the Northern Territory. Tony is an occasional contributor to *The Big Issue*.

GROWING PINEAPPLES IN THE OUTBACK

Rebecca Lister and *Tony Kelly*

UQP

First published 2020 by University of Queensland Press
PO Box 6042, St Lucia, Queensland 4067 Australia

uqp.com.au
uqp@uqp.uq.edu.au

Cover design by Christabella Designs
Cover photograph of the Lister family home in Mount Isa, with Diana's
green recliner on the front verandah, taken by Bronwyn Finch in 2016
Author photographs by Declan Kelly
Typeset in 12/16 pt Bembo Std by Post Pre-press Group, Brisbane
Printed in Australia by McPherson's Printing Group

  The University of Queensland Press is assisted by the
Australian Government through the Australia Council,
its arts funding and advisory body.

A catalogue record for this book is available from the National Library of Australia.

ISBN 978 0 7022 5412 3 (pbk)
ISBN 978 0 7022 6231 9 (epdf)
ISBN 978 0 7022 6232 6 (epub)
ISBN 978 0 7022 6233 3 (kindle)

For Diana

CONTENTS

Rebecca and Tony on the front verandah
of the Lister family home in Mount Isa

Perhaps Mum is coming do
days she's been withdrawn. No
the party, but by nature she is en
been as attentive as I could be: I'
out in the house and keep up
the go back in Melbourne. M
her, but she has spent too long s
I've tried to get her moving
I can understand her desire to
Tonight I watched her push he
eating anything. I couldn't ever
Mum's comfort food. Just befo
made her a cup of herbal tea. S
half-heartedly.

I open my eyes and see ligh
the bedroom door again – the
Mum never leaves the door o
when she finishes. I check the t

I stand outside my bedroo
lit toilet – the room is empty. I
then smell something odd – sw
some smallish brown blobs on t
closely, but bring my head up q
me gag. It's poo. I grab some to
I can and throw the paper in t
bathroom.

I walk back into the hall a
Closed. I turn and see that all
the lounge room. I think of D
Christmas tree! As I head up the

The lounge room is empty
Mum's chair. There's more on

PROLOGUE

Rebecca

I'm woken by the sound of the toilet door squeaking. I roll over and see light coming in under my bedroom door. I hear the door close and the light diminishes to a sliver. I know it's Mum. My husband, Tony, is away on a work trip, and Mum and I are the only ones home.

I look at my phone on the bedside table. It's 3 am but I won't go back to sleep until I hear Mum go back to bed.

I have been back in my childhood home in Mount Isa for just under a month. It's been thirty-five years since I've lived under this roof, but my ear tuned in to the familiar sounds immediately. As a kid, I could always tell who was in each room based on the sounds: the distinctive squeak of each brass doorknob, the *thunk* of the Bakelite switches, the rattle of the louvres in their metal frames, and the whir of vibrating venetian blinds whenever a door was left open.

In the first few weeks, Mum's nocturnal sounds and movements caused me to wake up instantly and dive out of bed to check

that everything was all right.
or three times a night, whic
was a bit like living with a ba
Georgina and Lucille, were re
cry and attend to them imm
I could wait to see what each
become more used to Mum's [
without alarm.

I roll onto my side and [
I can hear the neighbourhood
night. I don't understand wh
I was growing up here there w
those bloody mongrel dogs [
notice now. Perhaps for other
sounds of twenty-four-hour a
rumble of the mine that spraw
the sound of the road trains c
Barkly Highway.

I look at my phone again:
morning. I think about gettir
knock on the toilet door or
Mum has always startled easily

I also don't want her to fe
starting to fail, and she can oft
the toilet but then needs to g
She doesn't say anything abou
certainly interferes with her sl

I lift the lightweight doc
my shoulders. I should get up
system air conditioner. But I c
the doona up to my chin. I lc
when the bedroom is finally c

of kitchen paper and wipe the floor and chair. I throw the paper into the bin, wash my hands again and go to Mum's room.

When I open her bedroom door, Mum sits up and turns on her bedside lamp. 'What's wrong?' she asks.

'The toilet light was on, and there's blood on your chair.'

'I got up to get a glass of water.'

'Where did the blood come from?'

Mum says nothing. She looks pale and vacant. She lifts her hand to the back of her head, and then holds it up in front of her face. In the light of the lamp we can both see the bright red blood. She looks bewildered.

'Can I look?' I ask.

Mum shakes her head. She pushes back the covers and begins to get out of bed.

'What are you doing?'

'I want a glass of water,' she says. She stands and wobbles.

I reach out and grab her, saying she ought to stay in bed. She says she needs to sit up – she wants to go to the kitchen.

Slowly we walk down the hall, which gives me a chance to have a proper look at the back of her head. There is an open gash, bleeding. I think it will need stitches.

We get to Mum's chair and she collapses into it. I tell her that I'm going to ring an ambulance. She says she doesn't need an ambulance – all she needs is some water, and then she'll go back to bed.

As I stand at the water cooler, filling up a glass, I notice something stuck to the corner of the kitchen bench diagonally opposite. I look more closely: it's a small clump of white hair. Mum must have fainted as she was getting her glass of water, and hit her head on the corner of the bench on the way down.

I hand Mum the water and she takes the smallest sip.

'Can you remember what happened?' I ask.

'I was very hot,' she says.

I nod and wait.

'I came to the kitchen for a glass of water. I stood at the water cooler, and …'

'And?' I prompt.

'And I woke up on the floor.'

'How did you get back to your chair?'

'I crawled.'

'And bed?'

'I woke up in the chair and had to go to the toilet.'

I realise this was the sound I'd heard over an hour ago. If I'd realised she wasn't in bed I would have got up. I feel slightly guilty.

'And from the toilet to bed?'

Mum has no memory of that.

'Why didn't you call out or wake me up?' I ask.

'I didn't want to disturb you.'

This is Mum all over: raise no alarm, draw no attention, request no assistance.

'You had an accident on the way to the toilet,' I say.

Mum says nothing, but I can see her thinking. Eventually, she says, 'I think it was the camomile tea and the pear that you made me have.'

'A cup of camomile tea and a bit of pear does not cause someone to faint, split their head open and poo their pants!'

'Don't be so coarse!' she says.

I am relieved to recognise her fighting spirit, and happily correct myself: 'Apologies – soil their undergarments!'

Mum smiles, and this too is a good sign.

I tell the ambulance operator what has happened.

'Don't give your mother any water, and don't move her,' she says. 'Turn on the front light and make sure that the ambulance has easy access to the house.'

I take away Mum's glass of water; she barely notices.

I remember the poo smears in the hallway. I grab a bottle of bleach and splash it over the carpet. I get the kitchen paper again and rub at the mess. I know this is ridiculous. It's not as if the ambos are going to come down the hallway and do an inspection of the house. But I'm full of adrenaline and can't stop myself.

I grab a wet washer and more paper towel and try to clean Mum's feet, legs and the back of her neck and arms. I would love to get her into the shower, but of course that isn't going to happen.

Soon the paramedic, Jason, is kneeling beside Mum's chair. 'Can you tell us what happened, Diana?' he asks.

Mum has trouble piecing together what has happened.

'Is she often confused?' Alex, the other paramedic, asks me.

'No,' I say. 'Never.'

Alex says, 'Can we have a look at the back of your head, Diana?'

Mum nods.

Alex inspects her head. 'You've given it a good old whack, haven't you?' he says.

Mum nods.

'Did you feel any chest pain?' asks Jason.

'I don't remember,' says Mum.

'We need to check a few things – is that okay with you, Diana?' Jason asks.

Mum nods.

While Jason takes Mum's blood pressure, Alex attaches the sticky ECG dots to her chest, stomach and legs, and hooks the wires up to the monitor. Jason looks at Mum's eyes and tongue and does a skin pinch. They are both respectful and efficient, and I can see Mum slowly relaxing.

Even in the short time I have been with her, I've encountered a number of medical professionals who speak to her as though she is deaf and dumb. The ones Mum struggles with the most are those who call her 'darl' or 'love' – or even, believe it or not, 'babe'. Who in their right mind thinks it's okay to call a woman in her nineties 'babe'?

'Do you keep up the water, Diana?' Jason asks.

'I drink a lot of tea,' says Mum.

'What about water?'

'Yes, in tea,' Mum says.

I catch Jason giving Alex a quick smile.

'You're dehydrated,' Jason says.

'I try to get her to drink,' I say. I don't need to say this, but I want the paramedics to know that I take good care of Mum.

'Here's what I think,' says Alex. 'How about we put you in the ambulance and get you up to the hospital? You need a few stitches, and we need to run a few more tests and find out why you fainted.'

Mum nods.

'Do you think you can walk, or would you like a trolley?' asks Jason.

Mum pauses, then says, 'A trolley.'

This is significant, as Mum rarely takes up offers of assistance. If she can't see she might take my arm but that's about it. People who know her well know that she hates to be treated as though she's incompetent.

Jason and Alex get Mum into the back of the ambulance. She looks frightened; I don't think she's been in one before. I reach out and touch her leg and tell her she'll be okay. She gives me a little one-finger wave. As the doors close, I give her a one-finger wave back.

Jason gets in beside her and Alex closes the doors. 'Wait half an hour and then come up to the hospital,' he tells me.

'I haven't had a chance to clean Mum properly,' I say. I feel sad that Mum, who is always so groomed and meticulous, has to go to the hospital with poo on her. I hope she doesn't realise.

'Don't worry,' he says. 'She'll be looked after when she gets there.' He hops into the driver's seat and I watch them drive off.

I go back inside and head down the hall to Mum's room. The bleach I used has stripped the colour out of the carpet. I regret using it, and know that it will be an ever-present reminder of this event.

I pack a small bag of Mum's things in case she is admitted. I strip all the linen from her bed and shove it into the machine. I know it's crazy to be doing a load of washing at five in the morning but I'm wired.

At the hospital I am directed to the emergency department, and find Mum in one of the rooms. She is attached to oxygen and the colour has come back to her face. She smiles.

Over the next few hours she is examined, scanned, stitched, has blood taken, gives a urine sample and is asked to explain numerous times what has happened. With each new nurse or doctor, we tell the story again. Mum is given sandwiches, a cup of tea and a lot of attention. She is not given a shower or a sponge bath, and I continue to worry about this, but Mum doesn't seem to care so I let it go.

Eventually, a doctor tells Mum that she has a urinary tract infection. This is what caused the spike in temperature, the fall and the confusion. Mum is given a course of antibiotics. The doctor makes an appointment for her to see the cardiac specialist when he's next in town. She thinks there are problems with Mum's blood pressure, and her medication may need to be altered.

The doctor talks to her about dehydration and how important it is to drink enough throughout the day. Mum agrees with everything the doctor says and promises to drink more water. I have my doubts about this but say nothing.

One of the nurses picks up Mum's chart, reads it and says, 'Were you really born in 1924?'

'Yes,' says Mum.

'That makes you …'

'Ninety-one,' says Mum.

'Yes, ninety-one, wow! You don't look like you're ninety-one,' the nurse exclaims. I watch Mum sit up a fraction straighter in the bed and fluff up her recently permed hair.

'What's your secret?' says the nurse.

'Lots of water,' says Mum, and she smiles at me and I roll my eyes.

Later, at home, Mum has a shower and I phone Tony and the family to fill them in. I want Mum to lie down and rest, but she doesn't want to. She wants to talk. The antibiotics appear to be working, and for one who has had virtually no sleep Mum is extremely perky.

She tells me about her conversation with Jason in the ambulance. 'I apologised for the fact that they had to come to the house at such an early hour of the morning,' she says. 'Jason told me I was an excellent patient, and that many of their early-morning calls are for people who are drunk or have been involved in brawls. I was very pleased to inform them that I was both sober and non-violent!'

I just smile and nod. I am exhausted, and acutely aware that I should get back to work, but Mum is on an oxygenated high and I don't want to leave her.

'I have been feeling unwell for a few days,' she says.

'Why didn't you say anything?'

'I didn't want to disturb you.'

I think about how much time I have actually wasted over the last few days, and that perhaps I really needed a genuine disruption.

I spend the next few hours talking with Mum and doing a crossword. Her 'outing' seems to have done her the world of good. I don't get any work done, but I can work later.

In the late afternoon, my niece Belinda and her daughters, Madlyn, Ashley and Jorja – Mum's great-granddaughters – come over. They bring flowers and chocolates. A short time later, Samantha, Mum's other Mount Isa granddaughter, arrives. She brings more chocolates and flowers. The atmosphere is almost festive, and Mum sits in her chair, surrounded by all of us, and laps it up. She regales us with the story of the fall, the paramedics, the nurses and doctors, and the early-morning activities of the hospital. Though I detect a slight edge of embellishment, her capacity to recall all the details is spot on.

At this moment I am filled with a sense of absolute clarity. I am in the right place, at the right time, doing the right thing. I still have so much to sort out, and although that worries me, I know that this is exactly what I am here for – this is my purpose. Everything else is insignificant.

1

HOMECOMING

Rebecca

I come in from watering the garden. It's only 8 am but I'm already sweating. 'It's gunna be a hot one,' I say to Mum, but she doesn't respond.

Mum is sitting in her recliner, having her standard breakfast of one Weet-Bix with warm water and a tepid cup of milky tea. She is listening to Radio National and probably can't hear me. Tony and I have both noticed that her hearing is going. We also think that she may occasionally have a touch of 'selective listening', especially early in the day. I get it. She's lived alone for twenty years. She's adapted to not speaking to anyone in the mornings, but I've been up since 6 am and am ready for a chat.

Tony has already gone to work. He was up early too and went to the pool to do his laps. I was going to join him but wanted to get the watering done. The water restrictions mean you can only water your garden for a couple of hours every second day, in the early morning or late afternoon. No one in their right mind would want to water at any other time anyway.

We've established a routine: hand-watering in the morning and late afternoon and putting the sprinkler on the lawn after dark. Lots of people have put in household irrigation systems, but not us. Dad started using the hose and sprinkler in about 1956 and we're maintaining the labour-intensive system. We move the sprinklers every fifteen minutes over a two-hour period. I often feel like I'm channelling Dad when I'm on sprinkler duty. 'Better move the bloody sprinkler,' I'll say as I get up and meander outside.

Other than basic maintenance, the garden has been neglected for the past twenty years. Tony and I are trying to bring it back to life but it's hard work. It's incredibly hot, and the soil here is dust-like on top and clay-like below. We've planted a number of local native bushes but our success rate isn't good: we've lost over half of them.

'What's the plan for today, Mum?' I ask.

'Hang on,' she says, 'just let me turn this down.' She leans over and fumbles with the radio.

I praise Radio National every day. It's Mum's link to the outside world. She's always taken a broad interest in things but her failing eyesight has limited what she can read or watch on television. So RN – or Regional News, as Mum likes to call it – is a godsend.

I walk over to where she is sitting. 'Want me to do it?' I say.

'No,' she says, 'I am perfectly capable of turning down the volume on a wireless.'

I smile. Though Mum has handed over virtually the entire running of the house to Tony and me, she is still the boss of the radio. I go back to the kitchen.

'I'm going into town to do the shopping,' Mum says.

'Do you want me to drive you?' I ask.

'No, I've booked the bus.'

Mum uses the community health centre bus to get to many of her activities. She likes the independence it gives her.

I have recently discovered that when you are sixty years old and engaged in less than thirty-five hours of paid work a week, you're eligible for a Queensland government 'Seniors Plus' card. In less than eight years, I realised, I could be eligible for the card and then I'd be able to ride on the bus with Mum. I had a vision of us both sitting on the bus, in matching outfits, singing along to Johnny Cash! This filled me with a sense of both horror and amusement. I told a couple of my friends, who promised that if this ever happened, they'd come out to Mount Isa and rescue me.

'You need to write out a shopping list for me of what you want,' says Mum.

'What *we* want,' I say.

'I was using "you" in the plural,' she replies.

'And including yourself?' I ask.

Mum says nothing.

'It's the shopping for all of us, Mum – Tony, you and me.'

'I'll just fit in with you pair,' she replies.

'You don't have to *fit in* with us, Mum,' I say. 'We live together, the three of us.'

Mum says nothing.

'It's not me and Tony running the show, and then over in the corner, in the giant recliner, is poor old Mother, who has no say in things and just has to "fit in".'

Mum laughs but says nothing.

I sit at the table, eat my breakfast and write the shopping list. In some ways, I suppose, it *is* a shopping list for Tony and me. Apart from a few batches of biscuits, the occasional fruitcake and a corned beef, Mum no longer cooks. Tony and I do all the cooking and the housework.

When we first arrived, we were worried that Mum might feel besieged. Lots of our friends gave us warnings: 'Your mum won't want you taking over … Your mum will still want to control the kitchen … Your mum won't be able to let go …' Fortunately, things haven't turned out like that. I think the moment Mum saw us swing into the driveway, she pulled the lever on her recliner, put her feet up and handed over the reins of all things domestic. Other than a few niggly words here and there, we have set up a very compatible and companionable household. Mum has told me it was a relief, after almost seventy years of running a house and cooking meals, to hand it all over.

'I also have a doctor's appointment this afternoon,' Mum says.

Since Mum's fall earlier in the month, we've been having more regular check-ups of her blood pressure and heart.

'Do you want me to drive you to that?' I ask.

'Yes, please,' says Mum, 'and I'd like you to come into the appointment with me.'

'Okay.'

We sit for a moment in silence, and then Mum says, 'You're not going to wear that outfit, are you, to the doctor's surgery?'

I look down at my soccer shorts. I bought them at a sports shop in Mount Isa when we first arrived. They are baggy and cool, and they go perfectly with my old singlet with the pineapple on it. This pairing is currently my favourite ensemble.

'I'll add a pair of rubber thongs to complete the look,' I say.

Mum laughs.

A little later she and I sit together on the verandah and wait for the bus. It's at least twenty minutes until the designated arrival time, but Mum likes to be out the front nice and early. We do a crossword while we wait.

The bus pulls up and Reg, the driver, gets out. He opens our front gate and comes up the path. Nicole, a community support worker from the health centre, slides open the side door of the bus and gets the little steps ready for Mum.

'Morning, Mrs Lister; morning, Beck,' says Reg.

We both say good morning.

'Hot enough for youse?' he says with a smile.

'Yep,' I say, 'hot enough for me, that's for sure.'

'Bit of a change from Melbourne, ay?' says Reg.

'Yep,' I say, 'bit of a change all right!'

'Must be nice having your daughter back, Mrs Lister,' says Reg as he puts his arm out for Mum. She takes his arm and they head down the path.

'No complaints from me, Reg,' says Mum. 'No complaints at all.'

'That's good to hear,' says Reg. 'And how about you, Beck? Any complaints from you?'

'No, Reg,' I say with a grin. 'No complaints from me either.'

Nicole helps Mum onto the bus and into her seat. She is the first person on the bus this morning. She'll like that. She likes being in the front seat and saying hello to everyone as they get on. Reg closes the door and gets into the driver's seat. The bus moves off and I wave but Mum doesn't see me. She's deep in conversation with Reg and Nicole.

I stand on the verandah and look out across the front yard to the park and small rocky hill beside our house. Everything about this view is completely familiar: the red of the rocks and soil, the parched beige of the grass and the brilliant sweep of endless blue sky. I always knew I would come back here; it was just a matter of when.

It would be easy to write that our decision to come to Mount Isa was a wholly altruistic one, and that I'm as close to the perfect daughter as you can get. But that would not be the truth. The decision did come from a place of considerable love and care, but it was not an entirely conscious decision. It kind of snuck up on me, and before I knew it I was here.

Mum turned ninety last February. To celebrate her birthday, twenty-three family members gathered for the weekend at a resort in Townsville. I knew as soon as I saw Mum at Townsville airport that her eyesight wasn't good. I watched my niece Samantha wheel her into the arrivals area. Everyone was very excited to see each other, but Mum looked tired and withdrawn. She said she was fine and that it was just her eyes making her look tired. Mum has macular degeneration and her eyes often look sore. On that day one was red and slightly sunken, and the other was weepy.

But it was more than her eyes. Her whole demeanour was flat. Mum has an open, wide and smiling face and usually lights up when people speak to her, but she seemed almost disengaged when greeting family members. Samantha and Belinda both noticed it, but we put it down to Mum being a bit nervous or shy about the fuss being made for her birthday. The event was the only time I could remember us celebrating Mum's birthday as a family. I knew she would be feeling some social pressure so I was prepared to let things roll.

In all other ways she looked exactly as she always did. She was wearing smart light-green linen pants with a loud green floral shirt. Like many Queenslanders, Mum has always favoured large, colourful bird or floral prints. The bigger the hibiscus, the happier Mum is. On the collar of her blouse was her Mothers' Union pin. Her hair, which she had stopped tinting many years ago, was set in its usual curled style, and lacquered into a high, crispy wave. I knew she would have a set of rollers in her luggage so that she could 'freshen up her do' over the weekend. Her skin looked smooth and, for someone her age, relatively unlined. Mum has always been an advocate for sun protection. She's always worn a hat, and when she was younger she would often use an umbrella when out in the sun. I hated it when she walked around with her umbrella but, after thirty or more years of having skin cancers regularly removed from my face and body, I can now see the advantages.

As I helped Mum unpack her suitcase, I noticed that her luggage and some of her clothing was smeared with make-up.

'Where?' she asked.

I showed her the smears.

'I can't see it,' she said.

'It's everywhere,' I replied.

Mum looked closer. 'You're exaggerating.'

I said nothing more. It was evident that she couldn't see the marks.

When she was out of the room, I took her clothes into the bathroom and wiped off as much of the make-up as I could with a damp washer. I put a few items in the washing machine.

Mum came into the bathroom. 'Have you got the washing machine on?' she asked.

'Just thought you'd like the comforting sound,' I said.

Mum looked at me and we both smiled. We share the same little affliction in regard to washing. We both believe that, even when everything is in a state of disarray, getting a load of washing on restores a certain calm.

'You know they say that excessive washing is a sign of guilt?' Mum said.

I smiled and nodded. This is something she has been saying for years. When I was a kid, she used to pretend to be Lady Macbeth and rub her hands and say, 'Out, damned spot! Out, I say!' In her best schoolteacher voice she would tell me that Lady Macbeth's sense of guilt came from her involvement in the death of King Duncan.

'What do you think your guilt is, Mum?' I asked.

'Living so long!' she replied, smiling.

I knew it was a joke but even so I sensed a touch of sadness. I couldn't help but wonder if perhaps her life out in Mount Isa was starting to wear her down.

On the morning of the party, Mum surprised me by announcing: 'I don't think I can walk to the function room. It's too hot and humid.'

It was no problem to drive Mum from our unit to the reception centre. Aunty Eileen, who was ninety-seven, was also reluctant to walk, so she too was chauffeured. Aunty Mary, a spring chicken at a mere eighty-eight, chose to walk.

Mum was the star of the party and rose to the occasion. She was gracious and elegant, relaxed and happy. The food was great, the speeches funny yet moving, and we all participated in a general knowledge quiz – which for Mum was the ultimate party game. Of course Mum won. The whole event went off without a hitch.

Nevertheless, over the course of the weekend she remained slightly withdrawn and disengaged. She was supposed to go and visit her brother and his wife, but on the morning of the visit said she felt unwell and stayed in bed. I started to wonder whether she might be depressed. I'm acutely aware of the difference between depression and an isolated period of flatness, and I didn't want to pathologise her behaviour, but a seed was planted in my mind.

On the last afternoon of the reunion, I had a few minutes alone with Mum. We sat on her bed and chatted.

'How's everything going at home?' I asked.

'Fine,' she said. 'Why wouldn't it be?'

I paused. 'We need to talk.'

'About what?'

'Have you thought about a plan?' I asked.

'For what?' Mum replied.

'For the next stage.'

'Of what?'

'Living in Mount Isa.'

'There is no plan,' she said.

'You're just going to stay in the house?'

'Yes. What else would I do?'

I paused. This was the moment I'd been waiting for. I'd been edging around this question for years, but each time I tried to raise it, Mum shut it down.

'You could move to the aged care facility,' I suggested.

'No,' said Mum. Her reply was emphatic.

'But what if you have a fall or something?'

'I'll wear a buzzer.'

'Housework?'

'I'll employ someone, if need be.'

'It's going to get more difficult,' I said.

'Do you *want* me to go into the old folks' home?' she asked.

'I want what is best for you,' I replied.

'And that is for me to stay in my own house, where I've been for sixty years.'

I sighed loudly, knowing Mum would sense my frustration.

'I'm too old, Beck,' she said.

'You could come to Melbourne and live with me and Tony and the girls,' I suggested. 'Or move to Mackay and live with David and Eden and the kids.'

Mum shook her head. 'I don't want to do that. I want to stay where I am.'

The conversation was closed.

After the party I returned to Melbourne and began my master's in writing for performance at the Victorian College of the Arts. I continued to work on various arts projects, and went about my city life. My contact with Mum went back to weekly phone calls. She always sounded chipper. After these calls, I felt that everything was, as Mum had said, fine. The sense I'd had in February that

Mum was in some kind of danger slipped into the background.

In August I headed home to Mount Isa for a short visit. I was thrown by how the house looked. Everything was, more or less, exactly how it had always been, except now it was dirtier and more cluttered, and there was a worn-out and dishevelled feel to everything. There was some sense of order, but between the order was chaos. Every surface in the house, bar the kitchen bench, was covered – books, cups, tissues, medicine bottles, eye droppers, envelopes, coins, magazines, you name it.

I knew Mum had organised homecare assistance to come to the house each week, but judging from how much she seemed to know about these workers, they didn't do much cleaning. Conversation and engagement is an important part of the job, sure, but I couldn't help but think that a bit more time on the old vacuum wouldn't go astray.

Everything felt just a tad grubby: the bathroom and toilet weren't as clean as they could be, the stove and kitchen benches had a thin film of grease on them, everything was dusty and there were cobwebs in every corner, under the table and behind the doors. The house seemed hot, tired and crowded.

I immediately thought about Dad, who had worked in the assay office at the mines for almost forty years. His approach to running a house had been that there was a place for everything and everything in its place. 'There's no other way to run a chemical lab,' he'd say. 'You have to be organised and methodical. You take something out of a drawer; you put it back in the same drawer. You run a house the same way.'

Mum's philosophy had always been far more laid-back. She would take something out of a drawer, use it and then plonk it down wherever she was. Her view was that homes were for doing things in, not looking at. There was always a sewing project happening on the table or something being built on the lounge room floor, or stacks of library books on bedside tables waiting to be read or returned.

But things had now moved to another level. Although Mum would deny it, I felt sure she had progressed to a form of hoarding.

I watched her closely, and could see that she was still managing day-to-day things like rubbish and bins; that wasn't a problem. It was more the fact that she had lived in the same house for such a long time and had not thrown anything out.

Due to her eyesight and the heat, she always had the doors, windows, blinds and curtains closed. The air conditioner ran nonstop. Rather than open a curtain to let in some sunshine, she would turn on the overhead fluorescent light.

I could see that she had carved out a path for herself that ran from her recliner to the kitchen, the bathroom and her bedroom. Every other room in the house was full of stuff, and the doors were closed. Out of sight, out of mind.

I ventured into her bedroom for a stickybeak. The floor was covered in plastic eyedrop vials and tissues. The end of the bed, chair and doorknobs were strung with washing; even more clothes were draped from the cupboard doors, and on every surface there were countless items that she hadn't put away.

'All you need to do is move a bar fridge and a little TV into that room of yours, Mum, and you won't have to leave at all,' I joked to her.

Mum laughed, but I could tell she didn't find it particularly funny.

I tried to make inroads into clearing away some of the clutter while I was there. I spent as much time as I could cleaning, but what Mum wanted was company. She didn't care about the house. She wanted to play Upwords, do crossword puzzles and go out for coffee and drives out bush. We did all these things, but late at night when she was in bed I would get out the cleaning products.

I made a general enquiry to the aged care facility. While I was on the phone to the manager, Mum called out, 'You can make an appointment but I won't be going!'

I put my hand over the receiver. 'What are you doing?' I asked her.

'I'm telling you I won't be going for a meeting, or to live there!' She stormed down the hall and slammed her bedroom door.

I was so surprised: Mum never behaved like this. She was the doyenne of good manners.

Finally we talked.

'I'm worried, Mum,' I said.

'You don't need to be,' she replied. 'I have everything under control.'

'What about Betty?' I asked.

Mum's good friend had recently been attacked in her home. It was an awful story. A young man came to the door and asked for a glass of water. He then pushed his way into Betty's house, hit her around the head and fled when she collapsed onto the floor.

'I keep the doors locked,' Mum told me.

'What about the man selling vacuums?' I asked. 'You let him in the house.'

Not so long ago a vacuum salesman had come to the house, and wouldn't leave until Mum bought a new vacuum. When she went to write him a cheque, he said he could only take cash. Mum didn't have cash so he drove her into town to the bank to get some. She then paid him and he left, taking her perfectly good old vacuum with him. When Mum told us this story, we were horrified.

'I don't like that you have to step over the side of the bathtub to have a shower,' I said. 'It's dangerous.'

'I'll get home help to put in some safety rails.'

'You have an answer for everything, don't you?' I said with a smile.

Mum gave a little grin.

'Are you lonely?' I asked.

Mum did not answer.

Dad died from leukaemia in 1996, and since then Mum had been living alone. On some level I knew that, for Mum, this was almost a luxury, as to my knowledge she had never lived alone before. I got the feeling that she enjoyed having the space to determine her own routine.

'I am not depressed,' she said, 'I know that for certain. But, yes, sometimes I am lonely, and sometimes ...'

'Sometimes?' I prompted.

'I feel sad.'

This was all I needed to hear.

A few days later I flew back to Melbourne, and Tony picked me up at the airport. 'We need to move to Mount Isa,' I said straightaway.

Tony nodded.

'I think we go there for a year, get the house sorted, sell it and then move Mum into the aged care facility or bring her back here with us.'

'Is that what Diana wants?' he asked.

'Not really,' I admitted, 'but if we're there with her we can do it slowly and methodically. She's lonely. I don't want her to live her last few years like that.'

'Okay,' said Tony. 'I'll ask around about work.'

'Great!' I said, and left it at that.

A few weeks later Tony told me, 'I might have a job in Mount Isa.'

'Oh?'

'That is what you want, isn't it?' he pressed.

'Yeah,' I replied as convincingly as I could. Of late, I realised, I had let the whole Mount Isa situation slide to the back of my mind. 'What's the job?'

'I met the CEO of a native title organisation that has an office in Mount Isa,' he explained. 'He told me they've never been able to recruit a lawyer there, and that he's open to a serious conversation about work.'

'Wow,' I said. 'What about your job here?'

'I spoke to my boss and he'll approve two years' leave without pay.'

I could feel my heart beating faster. I had said we needed to move there, but had I just been blowing off some steam? Did I really want to 'up stumps' and move back? It was over thirty-five years since I'd lived there. Also, I was having a fab time in Melbourne, and was just about to launch a small theatre company with one of my best friends. We had all sorts of projects lined up. Could I live in Mount Isa and continue working on them?

Our daughters had finished school and were doing their own things, so it felt like we were almost 'empty nesters'. But did I really want to become my mother's carer? Could I backpedal and say I'd changed my mind?

A few weeks later Tony announced, 'I got the job in Mount Isa!'

'Right,' I said. 'So I guess that means we're going?'

'Looks like it,' said Tony.

'When?' I asked.

'End of the year works for me.'

'End of the year it is.'

After this, things moved pretty quickly. I contacted Mum and told her we were coming. I explained the plan, and she was surprisingly open to it. I even picked up a sense of relief in her voice.

From my townhouse in Clifton Hill it all seemed so doable. Tony would have a job and I would continue to work on projects back in Melbourne, flying in and out. I'd also cook up some work in Mount Isa. I knew I had good skills and was very employable. Too easy!

Tony and I told the girls.

'You're going to *live* there?' Georgina said.

'Yeah,' I replied.

'Why?' asked Lucille.

'To look after Mum – you know that.'

'But can't you live here and do that?' Georgina asked.

'No,' I said.

'Well, don't get any ideas that we'll be doing that for you when you get old!' she laughed.

'That's the only reason I'm doing it!' I told her.

'They can live with you, Lu,' Georgina said to her sister.

'No way,' said Lucille. 'We'll be putting you both in a home.'

God, I thought, young people are brutal.

I told my work partner, Joanne.

'A year?' she asked.

'That's the plan.'

'But your mum's well, isn't she?'

'Yes.'

'You'll be up there for longer than a year!'

Joanne is an actor, theatre producer and palliative care nurse. She knows about the hard yards of looking after people. Although I told everyone that we were going for a year, already I suspected that it would be for much longer. I just didn't have the guts to say it.

Joanne and I drew up a list of projects and tasks, and scheduled some Skype meetings and phone calls in our diaries.

'I think it'll all be manageable,' I said.

'Except that I'll miss you,' she replied.

'I'll miss you too.'

Slowly the reality of the situation started to sink in. We began packing boxes of things we might need, like our camping gear, and organised to truck them up to Mount Isa.

We told other friends. Most people were full of praise, saying that what we were doing was virtuous. Others challenged us: 'Move her to Melbourne and put her in an aged care facility … Move back to Daylesford and get a good house with a granny flat.'

Lots of people asked me about my siblings – couldn't they take her? Why was it always women who ended up doing the work of caring for aged parents?

I am the youngest of four children, and the only daughter. My eldest brother, Michael, died in 1994. My next brother, Paul, lives in Jacksonville, Florida. He and his wife have three sons who are still in school. Paul works as an engineer for a company that does a great deal of their business in Mexico, so it simply wasn't possible for him to uproot his life and come back to Australia.

My other brother, David, lives in Mackay and works as a contractor in mining and construction. He has three teenagers, all in school, and his wife had only recently recovered from cancer. He was also in no position to uproot his life and move his entire family to Mount Isa.

The only other people who could possibly take on the role were my brother Michael's four adult children. The eldest, Belinda, is married to Seppo, and they and their three daughters – Madlyn, Ashley and Jorja – live in Mount Isa. They're very close to Mum and offer lots of support, but they work and have a busy household to run. Michael's youngest daughter, Samantha, also lives in Mount Isa. She's an electrician at the mines and works long rotating shifts. She and her boyfriend, Thomas, have a full life. Samantha is also very close to Mum, but it isn't her responsibility to look after her grandmother. Michael's two sons, Brian and Michael, live in

Toowoomba with their partners. They are carers for their own mother, who has a debilitating muscular disease.

To me, it was a no-brainer.

And so, on Friday, 13 February 2015, Tony and I pulled our newly bought second-hand Prius into the driveway of my family home in Madang Street, Soldiers Hill, and began the task of looking after Mum.

I sit at the table and make a list of things I need to do today. Living in Mount Isa but continuing to work in Melbourne is doable, but not ideal. I look at my diary and can see only looming deadlines.

I'm working on a set of treatment documents for the film adaptation of my play *Home for Lunch*. I haven't worked in film before and am finding the task pretty slow going. I have an excellent mentor in Melbourne but I feel self-conscious about how long everything is taking me. This, unfortunately, just slows me down more.

Joanne and I have received funding to do a two-week season of my play *HERE* later in the year, and it requires lots of production. We're also working on getting support for the development of a new project called *Resting Bitch Face*. I have made a connection with JUTE Theatre in Cairns, and will go there soon to do some development on my play *Hypoxia*. I also have work coming up later in the year with the Victoria Trade Union Choir to tour a play I wrote and directed for them called *I'll Be There*.

In between all this we're writing funding applications, organising the incorporation of our company, and making future plans. All fairly standard work for freelance artists, but the tyranny of distance does make things more difficult. Skype is good, and I spend hours writing emails and making phone calls, but I know that I'm missing some of the nuances that happen with face-to-face meetings and discussions.

In our first few weeks in this house, it had been impossible to do anything other than sort through the chaos and try to make ourselves comfortable. Tony and I moved into Mum and Dad's old bedroom – and their sixty-year-old bed. Although the mattress was fairly new, the base was well and truly spent. We discovered that it was held together with short pieces of rope and propped up with bricks. Each time one of us would move, something would slip and we'd sink into the hollow in the middle. After a couple of sleepless nights, Tony pulled the mattress onto the floor. 'Let's think of it as camping,' he said. We quickly bought a new bed.

The house is quite small, and Mum and her giant recliner dominate the lounge room. Tony and I both felt the need for a little 'space' for ourselves, so we set up a sort of cubby arrangement in what used to be the car port under the house. 'Car port' is probably too fancy a name, as it's just a dirt space between the house stumps where Dad used to park the car. The sides are covered in chicken wire, and around the stumps are workbenches with numerous bottles of screws and nails, old fishing line wrapped around faded beer cans and an extraordinarily large collection of burnt-out elements from old jugs. Mum and Dad were both products of the Depression, and though their methods of organisation differed, neither threw anything out.

We bought fake grass from the hardware store and used pieces of worn-out carpet to cover the red dust. We surrounded the entrance with a nice array of pot plants, and set up a small table, a couple of folding chairs and a bluetooth speaker. I found a collection of old tools and other metal implements and hung them around the space in what I think is a rather Rosalie Gascoigne–inspired installation. We named the space 'Dinky Di's' in honour of Mum, and retreat down there on the weekends to have a beer, listen to music or make phone calls to family and friends.

We'd also managed to sort through lots of things in the house to make it more liveable. If we were not doing activities with Mum, we'd spend our evenings and weekends sorting. I found it difficult to determine what was treasure and what was trash. 'All trash!' said Tony.

Some things frustrated me, like discovering that all Dad's clothes were still in his cupboard. 'Why have you kept these?' I asked Mum.

She had no answer.

I pulled everything out and bagged it up for the op-shop. We all lightened up when I found two old fifty-dollar notes tucked into one of the jackets Dad used to wear to the races. Sly old bastard, I thought.

I looked everywhere for Mum's old artworks – her ink drawings and pastel works. I looked in old suitcases and boxes, and went through drawers, but I couldn't find anything.

'Where are your drawing books, Mum?' I asked her.

'I threw them out,' she said.

'Why?'

'No one wants those old things.'

'I do.'

'They were amateur, underdone ... poorly executed still-life pieces.'

I was so disappointed. I love Mum's art and kicked myself for not saving some of her work years ago. I couldn't understand why she had kept so much rubbish and thrown out what I think are gems. To me, Mum was so good at everything, but to her own critical eye she was no more than average. Her lack of confidence has at times run deep.

I discovered that Mum had spread her clothes across every

wardrobe and set of drawers in the house. 'What's the system here, Mum?' I asked.

'The system,' said Mum, 'is freedom of choice.'

My choice was to ignore her.

We ordered a skip, and when the bloke delivered it, I instinctively said, 'Oh no, that's way too big! Do you have a smaller one?'

'I'll give ya forty-eight hours,' he said, 'and I bet you'll be calling me to come and pick it up, empty it and bring it back for round two.'

He was right. After two days the skip was full, and he came and emptied it.

My nieces and great-nieces popped in and out and looked at what we'd done. Like Mum, they were not so enamoured with change. This house had been a constant in their lives, and I had to be careful how I approached things.

'Oh, that's different,' one of them said when she saw how I had rearranged the kitchen cupboards.

Yeah, I thought, different from chaos.

I went to great lengths to explain that we needed to create order so that we could live here and care for Mum.

'What do you think, Grandma?' they asked.

Mum gave them the thumbs-up and said, 'Awesome!'

We all thought this was hilarious, but it was the only endorsement the grandkids needed. If Grandma said it's awesome, then all is fine. Though at times I would have liked it if they said, 'You're doing a fantastic job, Aunty Beck,' I knew that their compass points only towards Mum. Their own mum was not very attentive, and, without a father, Grandma has been the primary stable figure in their lives. I don't mind. I'm pretty thick-skinned and have other people to stroke my ego. My job is to look after Mum, and to allow the grandkids as much space as they need to be a part of it all.

The thing that causes the most tension is the air conditioner. I can't believe how much of my time is spent both thinking and talking about the cooling of this old four-bedroom fibro house.

There are two devices. The first is the 'swampy', which is slang for a water-cooled evaporative air conditioner. The swampy works by blowing air through cooling pads. It doesn't get as cold as the second system, the splitty.

At first Tony and I decided that we would keep only the swampy on at night. Its carbon footprint is less than that of the splitty, and so in our minds it was a more attractive option. However, swampies work best if windows and doors are left open so that the air can circulate and mildew doesn't grow. At night we close the venetians and the doors, but this causes an air lock to form and makes the venetians rattle incessantly. This drives us crazy.

The other problem is that the swampy is a large unit, with its main switch in the bedroom we sleep in. It has vents that blow cool air into every room in the house. The splitties, however, are individual units, and we only have these in the bedrooms and lounge. If I turn off my splitty and put on the swampy but don't turn off Mum's splitty, she'll have both the splitty and the swampy going in her room.

So we do what everyone does in North West Queensland: hermetically seal the joint and crank up the splitty.

I'm menopausal, so I have to confess that I love the splitty. It makes the bedroom nice and cold, which helps me sleep. Tony finds it too cold, and throughout the night increases the temperature. I wake up in a pool of sweat and change it back to arctic.

This goes on all night until Tony gets up, turns the splitty off, opens the bedroom curtains, venetians and louvres, and gets back into bed. After a short time of listening to the rattling of the louvres and blinds, he usually gives up, gets up and goes to the pool. Unable to bear the heat without some form of cooling device,

I too get up, make a cup of tea and begin the grand opening of the house.

I open the front and back doors, then the curtains, venetians and louvres in the lounge and kitchen. I turn the louvres to the best angle to catch any morning breeze.

By about 9 am the temperature hits the mid-thirties, so I put the swampy on and change the angle of all the louvres. By midday, with the temperature hovering around thirty-nine degrees, I succumb again despite my personal politics, shut all the doors, louvres, venetians and curtains, turn off the swampy and put the splitty on in the lounge room.

We leave it going until 5 pm, by which time I can no longer stand being cooped up in the house, so I turn the splitty off, open every door, window, curtain and blind and turn the swampy back on. By about 10 pm we reverse the whole system and whack the splitty back on. It's exhausting!

My niece Samantha installed the splitties into this house with her brother-in-law Seppo (a fellow sparkie). Mum loves telling everyone that her grandchildren installed them. I think they may have had some assistance from a friend who was a fridgie and another tradie, but in Mum's eyes this is irrelevant as it was her grandchildren who did the bulk of the work.

I find the way that Mum praises the grandchildren very interesting. When I was growing up, my parents barely praised me. This was not out of malice or a lack of attention, but more a sign of the era. There was a definite sense that praising children too much led to vanity and big-headedness.

I remember when Dad picked me up from the school dance in 1979. I was sixteen and in Year 12. One event at the dance was the crowning of 'Mr and Miss Mount Isa State High School'. I had been nominated for this award, and had spent the last few months raising money, and going to interviews and functions with the various 'dignitaries' from town: the members of the committee who would bestow the crowns.

I jumped into the Kingswood and slammed the door.

'Who won?' Dad asked.

'I did,' I said.

'No, you didn't!' said Dad.

'Yes, I did!'

'Really?'

'Yeah!'

'Must have been pretty slim pickings!'

Dad and I both laughed. This was his way of saying 'well done', and I didn't feel any sensitivity about his comment.

'What did ya win?' he asked.

'Twenty-dollar vouchers from the chemist and the bookshop.'

'Good prizes,' he commented.

'Yep.'

When we got home, Dad announced to Mum: 'She won!'

'Really?' said Mum.

'Yep,' I said.

'Goodness me!'

This was said like the news was a shock. Again, I took no umbrage.

Mum made a cup of tea and we had a piece of fruitcake and talked about the evening. At no point did anyone actually say congratulations. My parents didn't say congratulations – they did congratulations. Late-night tea, cake and conversation *were* the praise.

I hear the sound of the bus at the front of the house and go out to help with the shopping. Reg and Nicole carry Mum's bags from the bus and put them on the verandah for me. I carry it all inside and plonk it on the table and kitchen benches.

'Turn the splitty on, Beck,' says Mum as she collapses into her chair. 'Must be over forty degrees out there now.'

I shut the house up, turn the splitty on and unpack the shopping bags. I am slowly introducing Mum to not using plastic bags. I take out a bunch of bananas that she has put in a plastic bag and think about saying something but let it go.

She's had a good trip into town but is exhausted. I give her a glass of water and make a cup of tea. She sits in her chair and watches me put the shopping away. 'You're so fast,' she says.

I just smile.

'It used to take me all day to put the shopping away,' she adds.

Tony comes home and we make lunch and do a crossword together. Mum is very good at crosswords, but as a threesome we are formidable.

We have some time to kill before going to the doctor. Mum asks me to read an article to her from the latest *Monthly* magazine. Whenever I read to her I use my best 'speech and drama' voice. Today it's an article about the economic growth of the United States compared to that of Australia. 'And surprisingly,' I read, 'the deputy assistant ambassador to the United States released this economic statement just after a highly contentious press conference in which he stated his emphatic support for polyamory, revealing that he and his wife had often had relations with multiple partners.'

I pause and watch Mum's face. Her eyes widen and her jaw drops. She looks at me and it tests my acting chops not to crack up. I hold this for a moment and then burst out laughing. Mum laughs too, but then says, 'Stop being so ridiculous and finish the article.'

I change out of my shorts and singlet and put on a dress in preparation for Mum's trip to the doctor.

'That looks nice,' she says. 'You should dress like that more often.'

I wonder at what age mothers stop commenting on their children's clothes, but say nothing.

I get Mum into the car and off to her appointment. As we drive we discuss plans for dinner. 'You could make that nice spinach and feta pie,' says Mum.

'You could help me,' I say.

Mum pauses, then says, '*We* can make that nice spinach and feta pie.'

We laugh and get on with the rest of our day.

2

BUSHED

Tony

'How many spares you carryin', Tony?' Buddy asks as we drive south out of town in the pre-dawn gloom.

There are termite mounds dotted in among the scrub. A trend over the last couple of years has been to drape old clothes over the mounds – a white shirt here, a red skirt there. In the half-light I can almost imagine them as people farewelling us on our expedition. I think of Burke and Wills embarking on their ill-fated mission, which passed not far to the east of here, over one hundred and fifty years ago. The streets of Melbourne had been lined with thousands of well-wishers as their cavalcade of camels, horses and wagons slowly edged north out of town. I worry that the termite mounds might be some kind of omen – perhaps our mission, though more modest, is similarly fated.

'One,' I reply quizzically.

Buddy's a local traditional owner, and he's agreed to take me, the new native title lawyer in town, and my colleague Neville out bush to see some cultural sites. He shakes his head. 'There's no way we can leave the road with only one spare.' He directs me to turn around. 'We'll get mine. This is a five lugger, isn't it?'

I remain puzzled.

'Five bolts on the drum that slot into the wheel,' he explains. 'Some have four or six, but I'm sure this is a fiver, like mine.'

I take his word for it and turn around. We grab two (five-lug) spares from Buddy's fifteen-year-old LandCruiser ute and start out again.

Beck and I have been in Mount Isa only a short time, and already I'm heading out bush. When she threw out the possibility of moving here, I immediately thought of trips like this. Out on country with elders, looking at sites and talking tactics. Now here I am – it's happening – but we're not off to an auspicious start.

The sun is just peaking up over the scraggly Selwyn Range when we turn off the bitumen onto Ardmore Station. Buddy has a big day planned visiting various sites across his country. The women in his family told him he shouldn't be taking us, as they are women's sites. But Buddy disagrees. I'm not sure if he disagrees that they are women's sites or that he shouldn't be taking us. For him, it's important that Neville and I film him talking about his country and plotting important places on the GPS, if ever his family is going to get a native title claim up.

We turn off the road and onto a dirt track that cuts east across the spinifex plain. We go through a couple of gates and past a bore, and then pull up at a granite outcrop. 'You only bring a woman here if you're planning on piccaninnies, if you know what I mean,' Buddy says.

There's one large rock with a ridge around its bottom edge sitting on top of another, even bigger rock. It looks like a penis; there's no mistaking Buddy's meaning. I suspect this is a women's site.

Buddy then directs us towards the distant hills. We pass an old mining lease with burnt-out trucks and empty beer bottles strewn across the red rocky ground. There isn't a scrap of vegetation. It's not even 9 am and it's already very hot. The picture's bleak: a field of failed dreams and hard living. Eventually we come to a dense gidgee thicket. Buddy tells me that gidgee wood burns for days. It also stakes your tyres, I realise, as the front passenger tyre deflates the moment we hit the thicket.

We get out of the car and inspect the tyre. It's completely flat. Buddy moves into the shade and watches as Neville and I work out what to do. Buddy's changed enough tyres in his day, and has clearly decided it's time for us city boys to get hot and sweaty. The ground burns my skin and sweat drips into my eyes as I dig out under the axle and slide the jack in. LandCruiser tyres are almost twice the size of normal car tyres. Getting the flat one off is easy enough, but Neville and I, with our skinny arms, struggle to get the spare on. 'If you get the angle right, one person should be able to do that on their own,' Buddy offers from the shade. I catch Neville's eye and smile. After a couple of goes we succeed and, after wiping off the dust and the sweat, we recommence our journey.

For the next five hours we poke around the backcountry, looking at geological formations and art sites. Faded yellow and brown ochre suns and snakes predominate. Each site has special significance to Buddy, and as the day progresses his stories get more and more elaborate. We're learning that Buddy likes an audience.

We come to a muddy waterhole at the base of some granite cliffs. Cattle have been in to drink and there's manure all over the ground; the water has a greenish tinge. I usually require very little encouragement to swim in any body of water, hot or cold, but there is nothing remotely enticing about this foul waterhole. We climb over the rocks to the base of the cliff and look at a series of ochre squiggles, standing in the blistering heat as Buddy tells us how he has tried to get money to protect these sites. As each year goes by, he says, the art fades more and more.

Neville and I patiently listen and film Buddy talking and pointing, and diligently plot the GPS points with the phone, but as soon as Buddy's done we race back to the air-conditioned vehicle.

'How you finding the heat, boys?' Buddy asks with a grin as he climbs into the car, having ambled back slowly.

No problem, we tell him.

By midafternoon I'm tired, and thinking we ought to start heading home. As if he can read my mind, Buddy directs us back towards the main road. But within a few moments he looks to the sun. 'Still plenty of time,' he says, then looks to the left. 'Turn here.' He flicks his hand but I don't see anything and keep driving. 'Stop the car – you missed it.'

I stop the car, put it in reverse and ease back along the track.

'Here!' Buddy points to two faint tyre tracks veering off to the left. I'm stunned by how well Buddy knows his way around what to me is largely indistinguishable country.

We follow the track as it winds through the scrub and up and down dry creek beds for miles. I'm ever conscious that we're getting further and further away from the main road. After an age we come across an eroded segment of track with deep wheel ruts. Worried that the car will bottom out, I try to drive along the top of the ruts, but in so doing break the seal on the wall of the front left tyre, the spare, and down it goes. I glance at the thermometer on the dash: forty-three degrees.

Without saying a word, we hop out of the car. Neville and I, knowing our roles, begin the hot process of loosening the wheel nuts, jacking up the front, taking off the flat tyre and replacing it with one of Buddy's spares. It goes on easily, and I rejoice that we had turned around and collected them.

We climb back into the car, and Neville, now behind the wheel, puts it into drive and eases his foot down on the accelerator.

The car doesn't move. I jump out and check the tyre: all seems good. Neville tries again but it still doesn't move. It quickly dawns on us that Buddy's old LandCruiser tyres, being thinner than the factory-fitted ones on this late-model vehicle, are incompatible with the braking system. Although they have the correct number of lugs and fit well, they won't go round. We are stuck.

Neville reaches for the satellite phone. He punches in the phone number for the station manager, which Buddy knows by heart. Nothing. We try the Dajarra police; nothing. My legs start to shake. Trying to maintain my composure, I read the satellite phone manual and realise we need to put in the country and area codes first. Dutifully we dial the numbers, but all we get is a recorded message: 'Your call could not be connected; please check the number and try again.'

We consider our options. It's too far to walk out, and way too hot. It'll be dark in four or five hours so it looks like we'll have to spend the night in the car. At least we have plenty of water. Neville and I look at each other gloomily.

I reread the manual carefully. Abandoning the cool of the vehicle, I get out, move away to avoid interference, make sure the aerial's pointing directly up and continue to try the numbers. After half a dozen attempts I get onto the station manager's wife, but by the time we can explain our location the line goes dead. I wait a couple of minutes and try again. This goes on for another twenty minutes until I get a long enough connection for Buddy to describe where we are. She says her husband is out mustering but she'll get onto the police.

Not entirely convinced she knows exactly where we are, or that the police will be able to respond to our mayday, we sit and wait. I put in a call to our colleague Kylie back in Mount Isa, and when I eventually get through I ask her to ring Rebecca. I know she and Diana will be starting to get worried. I'm beginning to realise that going out bush in this part of the world, especially at this time of year, is a big deal, and when you don't return on time people get worried. People get stuck out here and die.

We have plenty of fuel so we leave the engine running and sit in the air conditioning. It's still murderously hot outside and the flies are thick. We try jokes and some music, but Neville and I are too tense to embrace either. Buddy seems relaxed. He's been stuck out here a number of times and seems prepared to sit and wait, and even to walk out if no one comes. We keep looking to the west to see if a car is coming. After an hour and a half Neville reckons he can see the dust cloud from a car in the distance but nothing comes of it. We continue to wait.

'Why'd ya move here?' Buddy asks.

'To look after my mother-in-law,' I tell him. He asks me her name. 'Diana Lister. Her husband, my father-in-law Ted, worked in the assay office at the mine.' I also tell him about Beck's brothers, Michael and David, who worked on and off in the mine for many years. Buddy says their names are familiar.

We continue to talk about family, and I know Buddy's trying to place me. This is common out here. Everyone must fit in somehow, somewhere. I've seen Beck do it with her mum. Beck would mention someone she bumped into at the shops. Diana would probe until she got enough information to place the person. Sometimes it would take only five minutes, sometimes it would be an intermittent conversation over a number of days, until eventually Diana would announce it was so-and-so's aunty, and that she moved to Townsville years ago.

I suddenly remember that Beck's cousins grew up in Dajarra, the town Buddy's from. 'Do you know the Wrights?' I ask. 'Beck's aunty married a Wright. I think they ran the fuel depot in Dajarra.'

Buddy nods. 'Yep, they did.' Finally I'm contextualised.

'We were also ready for a change,' I add. 'We'd been living in

Melbourne for nearly a decade. Our daughters are old enough to look after themselves and we were keen for an adventure.'

'Well, you certainly got that,' Neville chips in.

'This is not quite what I had in mind.'

We return to silence.

What I don't tell them is that it's time for me to give something back to Beck. While I'm a very engaged dad and worked part-time when the kids were little to give Beck more opportunity to work and develop her career, she ultimately carried the greater burden in the career sacrifices she made for our family. Any time we were making decisions about jobs and places to live, we endeavoured to act honestly and with each other's interests at heart, but often it felt like the big decisions favoured my interests and my career. Moving to Mount Isa, at Beck's behest, gave me an opportunity to restore the balance.

I gaze out the window. The light is getting softer, making the orange of the dirt and the green of the spinifex richer. I wind down the window, thinking it will be cool, but hot air and flies rush in. I look up at the sky and notice some rain clouds gathering over the hills. 'Do you think it'll rain?' I ask Buddy.

'No, this won't 'mount to nothin'. We've missed the rain this year.'

We go back to waiting in silence.

Eventually, I see in the rear-vision mirror the glint of a police car coming through the scrub in the last of the light. The three of us scramble out of the vehicle as it pulls up. Out jumps a young police officer in shorts and singlet. 'Hello, I'm Dan,' he says with a big grin. Pointing to a woman in a cowboy hat and T-shirt emblazoned with an Aboriginal flag, he adds, 'This is Smiley.' Buddy knows Smiley. She's one of the women in his family who advised against the trip. They smile wryly at each other, but family business is not going to be aired in front of strangers.

Two more people emerge from the four-wheel drive twin-cab paddy wagon: Jessie and Clare, teacher's aides from the school, who've come along for the ride. Clearly we're the biggest thing to happen in the area for some time. Smiley tells us she has thrown a couple of spares in the back, hoping they'll fit.

'Five luggers?' I ask.

She shakes her head. 'Six.'

Bugger – there's no option but to get a ride back to town with our broken tyres and try to get them repaired. There's only room for one of us in the police car, so I farewell the others and squeeze into the back, next to Jessie and Clare. 'The roadhouse closes in fifty minutes,' says Dan. 'We'll have to hurry.'

'Your wife's Rebecca, eh?' Smiley says, looking at me through the rear-vision mirror.

I nod yes.

'She's with Feral Arts,' Smiley continues.

Over twenty years ago Rebecca ran a community arts project in Dajarra and the surrounding communities. I came along as a volunteer on one of the field trips. Smiley must have been a teenager at the time.

'I never forget a face,' she tells me.

We pull up at the roadhouse with ten minutes to spare, but it has the look and feel of a place closing up for the night when I slide open the front door. 'I need a tyre fixed,' I say desperately to the ancient proprietor, who is sitting behind the counter eating a bowl of ice cream. He glances at the clock – 8.50 pm – and then back at his bowl. He continues to spoon ice cream into his mouth. It's a line ball whether he'll help. He looks up as Dan comes in through the door, and I sense the balance tipping in my favour. Slowly he finishes his ice cream, then he climbs down from his stool and moves towards the workshop.

I'm flooded with relief. It's been a long day, and Buddy and

Neville are still sitting in the car with two flat tyres in the scrub forty minutes away. Not only do I have to get at least one of the two flats fixed, but I still have to get back out there and get the car moving again before we can begin the journey home.

The old man runs his hands around the tyres. After an age he looks up. 'Both of these are shot. There's no way they can be repaired.' He glances at Dan, the copper. 'I wouldn't be allowed to, anyway. Not roadworthy.'

Knowing there's no way I can argue with him on this point, I offer to buy a new one.

The old man tells me it's unlikely these late-model tyres will be in stock, and the way he speaks makes me feel guilty for driving such a flash car.

I stare at the broken tyres lying on the workshop floor. I look outside and can see a row of mongrel dongas illuminated by a lone flickering fluorescent light. That's where we'll be spending the night.

Taking some pity on me, the old man offers to have a look in the back shed. Another age later he reappears, shaking his head. 'Perhaps in this one.' He points to the shed next to the workshop. 'But first the keys.' He disappears again.

Unhurried, he returns with keys and a torch. Upon opening the door, he shines his torch on the closest tyre. 'This should do it.' It's a 285/65R17, and apparently that's just what we need. Then he begins the excruciatingly slow process of putting the tyre on the rim. I can't bear to watch, so I go inside the roadhouse to see if I can rustle up a couple of sandwiches to take back to the others.

I also take the opportunity to ring Beck. 'I think we're going to be okay,' I tell her.

'Good,' says Beck. 'Mum's been driving me crazy. "When will the men be home?" she keeps asking.'

I laugh. 'Tell her this man will be home after midnight. I hope.'

I can imagine Diana sitting in her green recliner, pestering Beck. At first she would have been excited for me, and curious, then as the day progressed she'd have become more and more anxious. After a lifetime in Mount Isa, she knows that being stuck in the bush in this heat is no small thing.

Finally the tyre is sorted and I follow the old man to the cash register. He perks up as I hand over $350 and starts on a conversation. 'Where you from?'

'Melbourne,' I tell him.

'Melbourne, eh? I like Melbourne. I took a drive there myself once. Went to Mildura, and from there we went south to Horsham, and from there ...'

I've been up since 5 am, have spent the whole bloody day poking around in the scrub, it's still hot, it's late, and I have a car with two people in it stuck somewhere up a track god knows where. I don't care about his Victorian road trip. Nonetheless, I take a breath and smile. This is part of the deal, I realise, the unspoken contract I entered into the moment I walked into his store. I let the story come to a natural end, then thank him for his assistance and go outside to see if my rescuers are still around.

Dan and the crew are waiting for me in the paddy wagon, having already stowed the new wheel in the back. After I cram myself in next to Jessie and Clare again, we head back out into the night. Forty minutes later we pull up behind Neville and Buddy, who are still sitting in the car with the engine running. They greet us with broad grins.

We easily get the wheel on, and this one goes round when the accelerator is pressed. So without any more fuss, and as we eat the best-tasting sandwiches, we follow the others back onto the main road and then turn our noses towards Mount Isa.

It's well after midnight by the time I get my first glimpse of the red light blinking on top of the lead smelter stack. The tall grey chimney that reaches two hundred and seventy metres into the sky, spewing fumes day and night, is Mount Isa's landmark. No matter from which way you approach the town, it is this stack that comes into view first. Next is the copper smelter stack, more benign at half the height, followed by the chimney from the sulphuric acid plant, which is smaller yet again. Finally, the full bestial body of the mine itself, stretching from the south to the north along the western edge of the town, emerges out of the dark.

It's an extraordinary monolith, and beautiful by night, when it's lit up like a carnival ship. By day its stark industrial ugliness cannot be disguised, surrounded by dust and toxins, radiating heat and noise. The first time I saw these lights was twenty-four years ago, when I flew in to spend my first Christmas with Rebecca's family. Then I had a ticket with a fixed return date. But this time, I realise as we creep into town in the middle of the night, I have no such ticket. This time I am here to stay.

I drop Buddy at his place and Neville back at the motel. I swing into the backyard of Madang Street and kill the engine. The house is quiet. Diana and Beck would have sat up as long as they could, eager to see me pull into the drive, eager to hear the stories, eager to know I'm okay.

Beck stirs when I crawl into bed. 'You're home,' she mutters.

'I guess I am.'

3

HUMMING ALONG

Rebecca

It's late afternoon and Tony and I are preparing dinner. I can hear Mum humming in the shower. She came home singing from church this morning. As the afternoon wore on, it shifted to her regular hum.

Tony and I catch each other's eye and smile. Tempting as it is to find humour in Mum's warbles, it is such a happy and unselfconscious sound that it's impossible not to smile. Mum is in good form.

I heard her on the phone the other day to her sister Mary.

'It's terrific,' she said.

Pause.

'Yes, Tony is an excellent cook, and Beck likes to organise everyone, but we have a lot of fun together.'

Pause.

'We do crosswords, and quizzes, and play Upwords.'

Pause.

'Yes, Mary, I highly recommend it – highly recommend it!'

I loved hearing Mum say that, and I have to agree. We are the three amigos. I knew we would be. We laugh a lot together. Mum and I have our own special humour, and though I know it becomes a little tiresome at times for Tony, I do catch him grinning.

One night we were sitting at the table, eating dinner. I held up a piece of roasted pumpkin on the end of my fork and said to Mum, 'I love eating yellow and orange vegetables.'

'That's very interesting,' said Mum.

'Isn't it?' I said. 'I feel like I'm eating golden goodness when I eat them.'

'I've never thought of describing plain old pumpkin like that!' Mum said.

'Once you start, you won't be able to stop.' I popped the piece of pumpkin into my mouth.

'Really?' said Mum.

'Yes!'

'Tell me more.'

'Well, my favourites are pumpkin, carrot—'

'Squash,' chimed in Mum.

'Oh yes, the often ignored yellow squash.'

'Ignored?'

'Yes,' I said. 'Like the carrot, the squash can often be found limp and lonely in the vegetable crisper.'

'Yes,' said Mum.

I continued: 'Capsicum, yellow zucchini …'

'Sweet potato.'

'Good one!' I said.

Mum did a thumbs-up.

We make little games like this stretch for a good half-hour, and each time we play they become more amusing.

I still don't have any secure paid work in Mount Isa, but have plenty on with all my Melbourne projects. I'm going to choir and keeping up my exercise, but I would like to meet a few people. Tony's work is going well, and although we both have our questioning moments we know that what we are experiencing here is very special. The girls are happy and well in Melbourne, though we suspect that our house has a permanent listing on a couch-surfing website.

The weather has shifted at last. The long hot summer was enervating, but the coolness of winter has lifted our spirits. The mornings and evenings are crisp, and the days warm and sunny. I love it and have been doing daily walks along the Leichhardt River. Seppo has given me a bike that he fixed up, and I'm having a great time riding around in the late afternoon and early evening. Tony and I are spending long periods of time in the garden; we've established veggie and herb patches, and the native shrubs that we planted earlier in the year are finally flowering. We've all noticed an increase in birds to the garden. Most days we spot rosellas, lorikeets, miners and butcherbirds. Mum can't see the birds anymore but listens for their song.

My phone pings and I pick it up. It's a text from Belinda:

The boys have just texted. They have left Cloncurry and the bus will get into the Isa in about an hour. C u soon! ☺

I text back:
Thanks! ☺

I tell Tony and he looks at the clock. 'I'll have the cake in the oven in the next twenty minutes,' he says, 'and then you can get the bread in.'

I nod and go back to crushing garlic. We both know that time is tight so we need to keep focused.

Mum has no idea that her Toowoomba grandsons, Michael

and Brian, are on the bus that will soon arrive in Mount Isa. They, along with Belinda, Samantha, Madlyn, Ashley and Jorja, are all coming over tonight for a surprise dinner. Mum thinks it's a regular Sunday-night dinner with just Tony and me.

This afternoon she asked me, 'What's Tony planning for dinner?'

Over the past five months, Mum has made it quite clear that she prefers Tony's cooking to mine. Most people do. She's happy enough to eat my food, but often starts conversations about meals with statements like this. Initially it irritated me, but I've stopped being bothered because I too prefer it when Tony cooks. He's a far more interesting chef and goes to more trouble to vary our meals, whereas I have a handful of tried and tested ones and roll them out week after week. Tony also takes the time to engage Mum in conversations about meal preparation, and involves her in the kitchen when he can. I get flustered when she's in the kitchen as I often interpret her advice as criticism.

Mum and Tony have an easy relationship full stop. This was not always the case. When Mum first met Tony, we had only recently got back together after a break-up. We were in our mid-twenties, and I, due to naivety or self-consciousness, had displayed an offhand ambivalence towards him. I didn't realise how completely in love I was until he called it off. Like many daughters, I went crying to my mumma and she propped me up.

When we got back together, Tony had to work hard to win Mum's approval. But he did, as he does with most people. He has a natural ease and gentle self-confidence, which means that people feel comfortable with him. He's non-judgemental and engages with people with a real sense of equality. Of course, like most people, he has an intolerance of dickhead behaviour, but overall he's always willing to accept people as they are. Over the years, in moments when I've lacked confidence, I've felt that all my friends end up liking Tony more than they like me.

Mum and Tony have been good friends for years now, but I did wonder how it would work out for all three of us living under the same roof for an indefinite period of time. Now, as I watch him drink his beer and prepare food for tonight's dinner, I realise there was no need to worry.

Mum lights up whenever Tony comes home at lunchtime and settles at the table with a new crossword. When he's away, she asks, 'When is Tony coming back?' When I drive her to church, she asks, 'Is Tony picking me up?' In fact, I'm starting to wonder if she, too, likes him more than she likes me!

'I'm cooking tonight,' I told her.

'Oh,' Mum said, and although I know she'd deny it, I definitely saw the slight disapproving twitch that she does with her nose when she isn't happy about something.

I considered telling her about our plan for pasta with pesto made from basil fresh from our garden, or the big pot of Napoli sauce that we made while she was at church, or the flourless orange cake that Tony has planned for dessert, but I felt that would give the surprise away.

'What are you making?' she asked.

'Vegetarian sausages,' I replied.

This time she made no attempt to hide it: the twitch of her nose was accompanied by a disapproving flare of the nostrils.

'What are vegetarian sausages made of?' she asked.

'Sawdust,' I replied.

Mum has eaten vegetarian sausages with my family and me for over twenty years, and she's always asked this same question. Initially I used to run through the list of ingredients on the back of the packet, but these days I offer a deadpan response.

'No, really,' she said. 'What are they made of?'

'Sawdust,' I repeated.

'Really?'

'Of course not! They're made of TVP.'

'What's that?'

'Textured vegetable protein. You know that!'

Mum nodded. After a short pause, she asked, 'And what's that made of?'

'Sawdust!' I said.

We both burst out laughing.

'What will you serve them with?' she asked.

'Mashed potatoes and steamed broccoli.'

'Make sure you steam the broccoli for long enough. Your broccoli is always undercooked.' Her nose twitches again.

Mum would never say something like this to Tony, and his broccoli is always al dente.

Mum's humming ratchets up a couple of notches. I recognise the hymn. It's one that Ash and Tara, local musicians who attend the same church as Mum, play regularly. Mum often comes home from church humming it. She sometimes gets quite demonstrative, clapping and waving her hands from side to side. It's an upbeat hymn reminiscent of the perky Christian rock numbers that Mum took a shine to in the late 1970s and '80s. Think 'Rock My Soul in the Bosom of Abraham' and you're on the right track.

Mum taught Sunday school on and off for years, and she would buy cassettes of children's hymns for her charges. She'd sometimes play them at home, but none of us took to them. We were all too old and into our own music. We had records, *Countdown* and concerts.

Paul belonged to a mail-order record club and every week something new would arrive: Uriah Heep, Led Zeppelin, King Crimson. I pretended to like these records but they were a bit beyond me. I was into the bands I saw on *Countdown* and heard on the rare occasions we were allowed to turn the radio dial from the ABC onto the local commercial station.

In my first year of high school I noticed that everyone wrote the names of the bands they liked on their pencil cases. I thought this was a very daring thing to do, so in a bold moment emblazoned my red plastic pencil case with all my favourite band names. I recently found this pencil case in one of my clean-ups and was horrified to see that I had spelt Abba incorrectly. There it was in thick black pen: ABAB. I was obviously not the sharpest pencil in the case.

My first concert was in 1971. It was a matinee performance with Jamie Redfern at the Irish Club. I wore light blue gabardine hotpants with a blue floral voile blouse that Mum had made. I teamed these with knee-high white socks and black patent-leather party shoes. Not very rock and roll!

On stage, Jamie told a joke: 'What's green and runs through the woods? Moldy-locks.'

I was star-struck. Here was a live performer who could sing *and* tell jokes.

By 1976 I'd seen Hush, the Ted Mulry Gang and Sherbet at the Mount Isa Civic Centre. Daryl Braithwaite even held my best friend's hand when he sang 'You're My World'.

So by the time Mum got into Christian rock songs, I'd well and truly moved on.

The family members who did love the cassettes she bought were Belinda, Brian, Michael and Samantha. From the early 1990s until quite recently, Mum had had the four grandchildren, and eventually the great-grandchildren too, over every Sunday for either lunch or dinner. When the grandchildren were kids Mum would play the tapes for them after lunch, and they would sing and dance around the lounge room.

Mum was beautiful with them. She loved children, especially

these children, and also music and dancing. Her grandkids did too. I don't know if they knew what the lyrics meant, but Mum always gave them her complete attention and they loved it. The joy of being a grandparent. Even now, when they get together, the grandkids often break out into an energetic version of one of the songs they learnt as children.

Mum's father was an Anglican minister, and the church has always been a constant in her life. Mum took as all to church as children, and we all got confirmed, but none of us remained connected to religion. Mum never expected anything, and there was no pressure for us to participate. Religion and church were very much her things.

Dad, a lapsed Catholic, was not particularly inclined to any form of organised belief system – other than those found within the unions, at the races and in the pub. On Sundays Mum liked to attend either the morning service or evensong, and Dad would chauffeur her to and from church. His other primary Sunday aim was to get to the pub. During the 1960s and '70s this was limited to two dedicated sessions: the first from 11 am to 1 pm and the second from 5 pm to 7 pm.

Before collecting Mum from the 11 am church service, he'd say to David and me, 'Want to go for a drive to the dump after getting Mum?'

We'd be in the back seat of the FB Holden before another word could be spoken. An outing with Dad was a treat, and we knew that once we were in the car there'd be no way he would change his mind and tell us to get out. Paul and Michael were both too old to be tempted by the excitement of a trip to the dump so were not invited.

Dad would load the rubbish into the boot and then drive to

the church to collect Mum. As soon as she saw us in the back of the car, she'd know what he was up to.

'I'm taking Beck and Dave to the dump,' Dad would announce, 'and then we might go for a drive.'

Mum wouldn't say anything, but her silence spoke volumes.

'I'll get them out of your hair for an hour or so,' Dad would continue.

Then Mum would turn and address us: 'Are you sure you want to go?'

We'd nod enthusiastically.

Turning back, Mum would say, 'Lunch will be served at 1 pm. Don't be late.'

'Don't worry,' he'd laugh. 'We'll be back well before then!'

I always knew this was highly unlikely, but I was an optimistic and obedient child and wanted to believe everything adults said.

When Mum got out of the car at home, Dad would say, 'You kids jump in the front with me.'

David and I would crawl over the seat to join Dad and sit three abreast on the bench seat. We thought this was the coolest thing ever. As we headed off we'd ask Dad to beep the horn and we'd give Mum a big wave through the front window.

At the dump we'd get out of the car while Dad sorted out the rubbish. The dump was a busy place on the weekend, and we'd often see other families poking through the rubbish. It stank and there were big mobs of hawks and crows and other scavenger birds hanging around, but it had a certain intrigue. Dad would let us turn over a few items with a stick, and then he'd say, 'Righto, into the car!'

'Where are we going now, Dad?'

Dad wouldn't answer, but when we reached the crossroad he would always turn left and take the road into town. I'd always be thinking, 'Turn right, turn right,' because that was the road home.

We wouldn't say anything but we knew what was happening.

Dad would drive into town and park the car in West Street. 'I gotta go and see a fella about a thing,' he'd say as he got out.

'What thing?' David would ask. He was always more assertive than me.

'A work thing.'

'Can we come?' David would ask.

'You kids stay here and look after the car. Don't get out.'

We'd nod, then watch as he walked down the street.

'He's gone into the Argent,' David would say. The Argent was a popular corner pub that had Sunday sessions. In high school I learnt that *argent* was French for money and Spanish for silver. I would think, 'Dad spent a lot of silver money at that pub!'

David and I have, as adults, discussed these outings. We'd never do such a thing to our own children, but back then we didn't question it. It was what it was. Neither of us have memories of it being unpleasant or feeling anxious about being left. There were lots of other kids sitting in cars on West Street so it was all quite social. Of course we'd get out of the car and play games on the footpath. We knew from experience that 'a trip to the dump' was code for 'go to the pub', but we craved his attention so were happy to play along. We truly believed that something more exciting might happen, but of course it never did.

What always happened was that eventually Dad would come out of the pub and take us home. We'd be late for lunch and Mum would be furious. Arguments would start about why he was late, why he'd been at the pub and why he'd left us alone in the car. I could never understand these arguments. Didn't everyone know what was going on? Why did everyone act so surprised and get so worked up by it all?

We kids hated these arguments, so eventually stopped saying yes to Dad's invitations to join him, and he stopped asking us.

Unfortunately, Dad's drinking habits didn't change and the arguments continued. We all learnt to live and operate around them.

It wasn't as if drinking and fighting were new to Mount Isa. At school there was a regular lunchtime cry of 'Fight down Wog's Alley!' and everyone would rush off to watch the latest punch-up. We sometimes heard people fighting in their homes or in the park next door. On Monday mornings at school there would often be someone who regaled us with a story of some kind of family barney. I never said anything about our family. I knew intuitively that that sort of conversation was off-limits.

From the outside we looked and behaved like any other working-class family. We went to school, participated in sport and arts events, had friends over, went to the pictures, played with our cousins and spent hours riding our bikes around the neighbourhood with other kids.

Inside the house, we learnt to plan around Dad and his behaviour. Friday night was the best night to have my friends around for a sleepover; Sunday was the best day to have a friend over for lunch and a game. Dad would happily drive me to my extracurricular events during the week, but on Saturday I had to ride my bike or get a lift with my friends' parents. Dad's Saturdays were dedicated to drinking, and nothing stood in the way.

When we were younger, Mum, like David and I, believed that his behaviour might change. When he'd say, 'I'll definitely pick you up from the swimming pool at five-thirty,' Mum would believe him. By 6 pm it would be evident that Dad wasn't coming, so Mum and us kids would begin the long walk home. Sometimes other families would offer us a lift but Mum always said no. She knew that Dad would be even more furious if we accepted a ride from someone else.

On the Saturday nights when Dad didn't come home for

dinner, Mum would take us in a taxi to the Finnish Café in town. Though I loved the ice-cold milk served in tall glasses and the crispy crumbed fish, I could rarely eat much. I was a perky kid with a cheery disposition, but at these meals my stomach would be a knot of nerves. I knew eventually there would be a price to pay for the taxi fares and the dinner out. My anxiety drew a veil across my ability to enjoy the moment.

Occasionally Dad would still do things like take us on picnics out bush. I think he wanted to do the right thing but he carried a social anxiety that meant he was unable to settle into events unless he had grog to soothe his nerves.

One afternoon our family was having a picnic at a waterhole out bush with my cousins and uncle and aunty. I watched Dad as he opened the esky and counted the number of beers inside.

'I'm going back into town,' he said to Mum.

'What for?' Mum asked.

'Pick up a few more beers,' he said.

'There's plenty in the esky,' Mum said.

'We might need a few more.'

Mum didn't say anything. She knew well enough to not cause a scene in public, even if it was just in front of her sister. Dad got into the car and drove away.

He was gone for hours and I remember watching Mum like a hawk. I was anxious and looked to her for cues for how I should feel or behave. But she gave nothing away.

'When will Dad be back?' the boys yelled out from the waterhole. 'When will the barbie be cooked? Do we have to wait for Dad?'

Mum pretended not to hear them.

The adults made the fire and cooked the food, and finally, after dark, Dad returned. He was rotten drunk but we all piled into the Holden and he drove us home. No one in the car said a word.

I hated the tense silences far more than the loud arguments. I knew they meant that something far worse was to come. At least with the arguments I knew the procedure. Michael or Paul would get David and me and take us out of the house. We'd go and play in the park or go for walks and return when they figured the worst of it would be over. But the silences could linger for days.

It wasn't that Mum disliked drinking per se. She didn't have a problem with people having a few drinks, and every now and again I would see her have a glass of beer or wine. But Dad's drinking meant he shirked his responsibility as a parent. Alcohol caused him to have a personality change, making him unpredictable.

So Dad would spend all Saturday afternoon at the pub, and Mum would spend it at home with us kids. She was no doubt tired, and sick of parenting alone, so her irritation would grow. When we saw Dad's car roll into the driveway, we'd say to Mum, 'Don't start anything.'

'I won't,' she'd reply.

The drunker he was when he came in the door, the greater her ire would be. There's nothing to be gained by trying to have a sensible conversation with a drunken person but Mum would forget this. Dad would try to be coy but Mum wouldn't have a bar of it. She would bait him and he would arc up. The tongue of an intelligent sober person is far sharper than that of a drunk, and Dad always felt the attack. His default position was anger, so then they'd be off.

I hated it. I felt sad and frightened. We all did. But then it would be over and we'd go back to being normal again.

Kids are incredibly resilient, but addiction and violence are damaging. When I first started to study social work, I felt for a time that the trauma of my family had left me wounded. But as I developed more knowledge, skills and experience, I realised I was not wounded. I was bruised and battle-weary, but thankfully there was always just enough love to keep us protected.

Mum once said to me, 'Your father's the sort of man who should never have had children.'

I knew what Mum meant, but still I felt loyal to Dad. Mum was loyal to him too, but she came second to his addiction. He never missed a day of work and always made sure we had everything we needed, but his drinking was always there.

Things did eventually get better, but not before getting worse. In 1971 my brother Michael disappeared, setting off an emotional explosion inside our household.

Throughout my adult life, I have tried to piece together what happened, but it has been difficult. Like many people of her generation, Mum believed that the past was exactly that – past. To speak about such things would do nothing but stir up sadness and grief. She felt that the best course of action was to let the past go and move on. I tried once or twice with Dad, but he made it clear that there was no way he would ever talk about it with me.

What I do know is that Michael was a greatly loved firstborn. Mum would tell me how she and Dad would sit him on the kitchen table dressed in his pyjamas and ready for bed. They would then bathe his feet in a little basin, and Dad would carry him to bed so that he could get into his sheets with perfectly clean feet. It always sounded to me that he was treated like a prince.

He was by all accounts a 'normal' kid. He went to school, played sport and hung out with his siblings. He liked cars and camping. He had an easy and confident disposition.

Michael finished Year 10 in 1966. He chose to join the army and do an apprenticeship as a fitter and turner. Throughout high school he had been involved with army cadets, and as Dad was a returned World War II soldier it must have seemed like a logical move. The apprenticeship was in Melbourne, so at the ripe old age of fifteen he was put onto a train and sent away. I had just turned four.

Early on during his apprenticeship, Michael absconded and was listed as AWOL.

Years later, Michael told Mum that the reason he ran away from the army was that he was lonely and scared. Mum understood the loneliness bit. He had been left more or less alone for a long weekend in the army barracks. Most of the other young men were from rural Victoria, and had gone home. We don't know what scared him but he took off and headed to the city. Becoming lost and disorientated, Michael didn't have the confidence to ask for help. I don't know how long it was before the army found him, but when they did they put him in a military prison in Melbourne.

Michael told my brother Paul that the army's main aim during his prison sentence was to break him. They saw his absconding as a weakness, and they told him they were going to break that aspect of him and make him into an army man. But Michael refused to break. Eventually the army dismissed him, saying he was 'psychologically unfit for military service'.

Michael was now free to do whatever he liked, and he chose to disappear. My parents did not know where he was. They contacted the army but they wouldn't help find him. I can't imagine what this was like for my parents, when their son was so young and naive.

After many months Dad received word from somewhere and went to Melbourne. He found Michael living quite close to the army barracks in a share house with other men and working on a rubbish truck. Dad brought him back to Mount Isa, and arranged an apprenticeship for him as a diesel fitter with Mount Isa Mines.

Paul remembers how changed Michael was. He had gone to

Melbourne as a shy bush kid and come back gung-ho and assertive. 'He was not the person I knew before he left,' Paul told me. 'I never felt comfortable around him after he returned. He had a bravado that lacked compassion.'

Michael completed his apprenticeship at the end of 1970 and then went with a group of mates on a holiday to the Gold Coast. While there, they all got drunk, drove a car through a zebra crossing and accidentally killed a young woman. I don't know who was driving. I do know that my brother bolted from the scene of the accident and went into hiding.

Again my father went looking for him, and eventually found him in Far North Queensland. Together they sought legal advice. This was at the height of the Vietnam War, the beginning of the Bjelke-Petersen regime, and a time of great fear in relation to police and legal affairs in Queensland. The lawyer's advice was that Michael should 'disappear' for the next ten years. He did, and was on the run for the next decade.

Like many people from that time who wanted to hide away or escape, he gravitated to the Gulf of Carpentaria and the Northern Territory. He worked on prawning and fishing boats, drove trucks and did stints in the mines.

Back at home, no one said a word. I had no idea what had happened or where he was. I was a chronic eavesdropper as a kid, so would occasionally pick up tiny threads of information from overheard conversations between Mum and her sister Veronica. But in the family no one said Michael's name or spoke about him. We did not acknowledge his birthday or his absence at Christmas or other special occasions. It was as though he had never existed.

Over the years, I've wondered if this decision to not speak about him was quite conscious. Did my parents actively encourage us to forget in order to spare us pain, or were they in so much pain themselves that they couldn't bear to speak his name?

I didn't ever ask Mum where my brother was. I spent an enormous amount of time with her, as Dad was largely absent too, but nothing was ever said. Like most kids of that era, I took my cues from the adults around me; if they didn't speak about it, neither would I.

Sometimes, when no one was watching, I would slip into Michael's abandoned bedroom and go through the items in his drawers. I found his army dog tags and his apprenticeship records. I looked at his handwriting and wondered where he was. I went through photo albums and found pictures of him. My favourites were one of him in his cadet uniform, and another of him wearing stovepipe jeans and a white turtleneck sweater. I would stare at these and try to remember what his voice sounded like, how he smelt and what his touch might be like.

One afternoon, a few years after he had disappeared, I came home from school and Mum told me to get my homework done quickly because we had a visitor coming for dinner. I asked who it was but she wouldn't tell me. After dark, the back door opened and a man with a big black beard came into the kitchen. I looked at him and felt something lurch in my stomach.

The man put his hand out and tapped the peak of my Skippy cap. 'Do you know who I am?' he asked.

'I think you're my brother,' I said.

'Yeah,' he said. 'I'm your brother.'

I remember his smile, and the deep urge I felt to know this adult, but the visit was short and before I could get past my shyness he disappeared again.

I recall seeing him again a few years later, but again the contact was covert and guarded. At the time he was driving trucks and snuck into town after dark. He parked his truck in the bush on the outskirts of town, and Dad drove out to pick him up and bring him home. I have no idea how Dad knew where to find him.

We didn't have a telephone, so I can only think that Michael rang Dad at work.

I remember Michael arriving with a large bottle of Coke. We'd never had Coke in the house before and I was very excited. Mum had made a popular new dip out of creamed cheese and a packet of dried French onion soup. As was the way in Queensland in the 1970s, she added a can of crushed pineapple to the dip.

I watched and listened as Mum, Dad and Michael talked. They weren't interested in either the dip or the Coke so I ate and drank the lot. Michael stayed till late and then Dad drove him back out bush to the truck and he disappeared again. I spent the next day vomiting up dip and Coke. I still find both hard to stomach; the smell always reminds me of that night. I have no memory, however, of what anyone spoke about.

Over the next few years both my parents' behaviour changed. Dad's drinking and temper became worse, and Mum began to withdraw. She stopped socialising, and other than doing things like the shopping and going to church, she more or less stayed home. She had always liked having people over for lunches and dinners, but these now came to an end. I think partly it was a self-enforced purgatory, and partly it was that she wanted to be at home in order to keep things as 'normal' as possible.

I do remember that this was the time when she started doing crosswords. In 1973 my Grade 6 teacher said, 'Everyone should read *The Pilgrim's Progress* and *The Thirty-Nine Steps* and do one crossword puzzle a day.' I went home and told Mum this. She got the books from the library for me but I wasn't particularly interested in them; I was too young. But Mum started doing a crossword every day, and she never stopped. In hindsight I can see that it's the perfect activity for someone who is somewhat isolated.

Dad came to rely more and more upon alcohol. The more he drank, the more unavailable he became – and the more unavailable he became, the more we wanted his attention, and the more irritated he became with us, the more he drank.

There were still times when he was just regular and normal Dad, when he was funny and solid. I remember one time when I was collecting the eggs in the chook pen. Mount Isa was a very multicultural town, and lots of my friends at school were bilingual. I remember asking Dad, 'Can you speak another language?'

'Yep,' he said, 'I can speak English and foul.'

I was very pleased with this answer and told all my friends at school that my dad could speak English and Fowl. In my mind he was the 'chook whisperer'. It wasn't until years later that I worked out he was having a joke with me.

Dad really liked company. Every Saturday morning, no matter how drunk he'd been the night before, he would wake up early and get us all up. His favourite way to do this was to come to the bedroom door and sing the famous lines from *The Barber of Seville*. He had a good singing voice, had studied piano as a boy and was quite musical. He'd shake the end of the bed and bellow out, 'Figaro, Figaro, Figaro!' until the whole house was awake and sitting at the table with him to eat breakfast.

We'd all think that it was going to be a great weekend, but by 10 am Dad would be preparing to head out. He was a creature of habit, and we all knew his routine. We'd be silenced as he listened to the scratchings on the radio. *Three-Way Turf Talk* ruled. Then he'd head to the bathroom for a shave and a shower. He'd douse his hair with Vaseline Intensive Hair Tonic, and comb it into place with his white plastic comb. For my entire life Dad always had the same comb. He was very proud of his hair, and it remained black and shiny until the day he died. Then he'd get dressed. If it was summer, he'd wear walk shorts, a short-sleeved shirt and leather thongs. He only wore rubber thongs if he was watering the yard. In winter it'd be long pants and a sports jacket. He'd emerge from the bedroom and his blue eyes would be sparkling. He'd virtually skip down the hall as he prepared to head out. I suppose he could almost taste that first beer. When we were younger, David would imitate Dad's jaunty gait and vain air, and we thought it was the funniest thing ever.

We'd watch the car back out of the driveway and then he'd be gone for the day. He'd go to the TAB, then the pub, then the track and then back to the pub. It wasn't unusual for someone to drive Dad home after a big session. Sometimes they'd bring him up the back ramp and into the house; other times they would just lift him out of the car and drop him over the fence into the backyard.

I hated when this happened. I would feel so embarrassed and ashamed.

Then out of the blue Dad would do something that made me feel like he was the best father in the world.

In the mid 1970s I started playing Monday-night basketball with a girl called Christine. She was a new friend from school, and we were having a wow of a time on the team. We both loved basketball and played hard. At one of the games our coach kept telling us to play 'man-on-man'. 'Stick to your opponent,' he ordered us. We both liked our coach and responded well to his instructions, but it drove the other team wild. They couldn't get past us, and one of them told Christine that they were going to 'bash her' after the game.

The coach told us not to worry, and after the game finished we headed outside the courts to wait for Dad. The girls from the other team were out there, and when they saw us they pounced – but it was only Christine they attacked. They punched and kicked her viciously. Christine was a tenacious thing and fought back, but this only made things worse.

Suddenly I looked up and saw Dad's Kingswood pull in. Dad leaned over the seat and flung open the back door. 'Get in!' he yelled.

I grabbed Christine and threw her into the back seat. Of course, as soon as the other girls saw Dad they took off. Christine clung to me and cried. It was awful, and she was embarrassed. I was terrified that Dad would be furious at us.

But Dad did not miss a beat. He just drove steadily to Christine's house. 'You okay, Christine?' he asked.

'Yep,' she said – and then, between tears, 'Sorry about that, Mr Lister. Those girls started it, not me.'

'I know,' Dad said. 'Some people fight on Friday night at the pub, and it seems like some fight on Monday night at basketball too.'

Christine smiled. When we got to her house, Dad asked if she wanted him to come in and talk to her parents. But she didn't. We sat in the car and watched her go in. I climbed into the front seat and we drove in silence for a bit.

'You okay?' Dad finally asked.

'Yeah,' I said.

'Tough game,' he said.

'Yeah,' I said, and looked across at Dad. He smiled and I smiled too.

At that moment I felt safe and protected. Dad had saved the day. He'd got us out of the situation and had not made a big deal of it. I had been scared that he might have wanted to go and speak to the coach or have a go at the girls who attacked us, but he got it – he knew that all he needed to do was look after Christine and me. And he did.

Fortunately, Dad's worst behaviour did stop by the time I was in my mid-teens. By then he was in his late fifties and had started to slow down all round. Also, by then we had begun to confront him when he behaved badly.

'You can't wear that top!' he said to me one night.

I was dressed to go to the pictures and was wearing a top with thin spaghetti straps. 'Why not?' I asked.

'Put a shirt on over the top of it.'

'No!'

'It's too revealing,' he snapped.

'It's the fashion! Just cos you're a "wrinkly" doesn't mean that I can't wear what I want,' I argued.

'Get a shirt or I won't drive you.'

'I wear this top every Saturday afternoon but you're too drunk to notice then, aren't you?'

'Watch what you say!'

'Or what?' I screamed. 'You'll hit me?' I raced to my room and slammed the door.

I was scared. I knew Dad wouldn't hit me. He had never placed a finger on me. My brothers hadn't been so lucky but I was his 'golden girl', and I'd reached an age where I knew this and pushed the boundaries all the time. I was scared he wouldn't let me go to the pictures or would refuse to drive me. I had a boyfriend and had plans to meet him, and I didn't want anything to get in the way of that.

Mum followed me, and I cried, 'Why is he like that?'

'You have to remember that your father hasn't had much contact with teenage girls since before the war,' Mum said. I couldn't help but smile at that.

'Put a shirt on. You can take it off when you get to the pictures and put it in your bag.'

I did as she said, got in the car and Dad drove me into town. Not a word was said, and there was Dad waiting to pick me up at 11 pm after the picture finished.

Like many women of her generation, Mum never spoke about or complained about any of the things that had gone on in our family. While on some level this capacity for stoic resilience is an asset, it can also set up patterns of behaviour that lead to emotional shutdown. Mum rarely let on that she wasn't coping.

When I was a teenager, she told me she had been to the doctor for her insomnia and had cried when he asked her how she was feeling. When she told me this, I was both too immature and too surprised to respond with anything akin to empathy. The doctor offered her Valium but she didn't take it. I remained mute and offered nothing.

Mum did start to emerge again during this time, though. She joined a few groups and started to volunteer as a tutor of English as a second language. She didn't do a course but got numerous books from the library and used her skills as a teacher to figure out what to do. She loved this work. Every week students of different nationalities would come to the house and Mum would conduct lessons at the kitchen table. Many of these students were isolated and lonely in Mount Isa, and Mum provided a motherly presence for them. There were frequent gifts of food, which we all loved.

In Darwin, in 1977, Michael met a young Jordanian woman called Julie. She too was on the run, escaping a traditional family back in Sydney. Later that same year their first son, Michael Pancho, was born. Tragically, while backing out of the driveway, Michael accidentally ran over his son and killed him. Michael Pancho was just shy of twelve months old. Four more children were born from this relationship, but by the time the last baby, Samantha, arrived, Michael was himself a full-blown alcoholic.

My clever, handsome but damaged brother didn't ever recover. In October 1994, on what would have been his first son's eighteenth birthday, he brought it all to an end and took his own life.

Within hours of learning that Michael was dead, I went into labour, and Lucille was born the next day. I was unable to get to Mount Isa for the funeral, but the day after Mum arrived in Brisbane to help me with seventeen-month-old Georgina and newborn Lucille. Tony and I were living in a share house with our dear friend Ruth. The house bulged at the seams with both life and death. Mum insisted on spending time every afternoon writing thankyou cards to people who had sent sympathy cards. Mum sat at the table and wrote and wept. It was awful. I told her she didn't need to write the cards immediately – she could wait weeks if she wanted, or even months or years. But Mum insisted there was an expected timeframe with these things, so she wrote and I wiped her tears.

How Mum ever finds anything to hum about amazes me. But hum she does. And I am so happy to be part of creating a household where, despite all her grief, she feels happy, and her humming survives.

I hear Mum get out of the shower and go into her bedroom. I need to get a move on with dinner, because if she comes into the kitchen and sees the mound of food we have prepared she'll wonder what on earth is going on. Although she doesn't know it, she's the star attraction of tonight's dinner.

Mum recently spent time in hospital after a heart attack. It was a sobering time for all of us as we faced the reality that her health was deteriorating. But from the way she described her five days in intensive care, it was as good as a holiday. It took us a while to leave on discharge day, as she had to say her goodbyes to all the ICU staff.

My nieces and I have often had a giggle about how formal Mum can be when thanking people. 'Thank you for your kindness,' she always says. We love saying this to each other, with tongue-in-cheek ceremony, as we hand each other a large glass of wine or an open stubbie.

But Mum really did want to thank everyone, believing they had given her care and treatment way beyond what their jobs required. She had connected with everyone – she knew where they came from, how long they had lived in Mount Isa and how they came to work in health care.

Within days she was back with her gang of buddies at church, and they all commented that she had never looked better. Each time I looked in the mirror, by contrast, I thought I had never looked worse. The tension of the week, my neglected work, along with the fact that I was smack-bang in the middle of menopause, had caused my insomnia to return, and the strain showed on my face.

I finish preparing the garlic bread and get it into the oven. Mum comes into the kitchen, and I'm surprised to see that she's dressed in her winter nightie, dressing gown, socks and slippers. I know she will be horrified when the family arrive and find her in her 'jarmies'. I also know she won't have the energy to get changed into other clothes for dinner. 'Don't you think it's a little early to get into your leisure suit?' I joke.

'I've recently had a heart attack,' she says, 'and I can wear my pyjamas at any time of the day if I choose.'

She moves to her chair and sits down without noticing the food preparation going on in the kitchen. I text Belinda:

Mum's in her pyjamas. She doesn't have a clue!

A reply comes instantly:
LOL!!! 😄

But I'm actually worried:
What should we do? 😕

Belinda isn't bothered at all:
Nothing! She'll be fine ☺

What feels like minutes later, the family arrive and pour into the house. Mum is thrilled to see everyone, but especially Michael and Brian. She can't believe they've come all this way to see her. 'One last visit to the old girl before she shuffles off,' she jokes.

We all laugh, but on some level that's exactly what this is.

The boys shower her with hugs and kisses. They are affectionate men and feel a deep love for their grandma. Mum glows.

I've always felt that it was the grandchildren who dragged Mum into the modern age of childrearing, where it's acceptable to kiss one another and say 'I love you'. I don't remember anyone's parents doing that when I was growing up, and mine certainly never did. I never talked about things like this with my friends, either. It wasn't until I left home and started to study that I realised the impact that love has on growth and development.

In spite of all the things that went on in our family, I never doubted that I was loved. But the idea that your parents would say it to you or express outward signs of affection when other people were around was a 'shame job'. I remember being mortified when Dad grabbed me in a huge bear hug at the airport in 1980 as I was leaving Mount Isa to go overseas as an exchange student. He'd had a few 'sherbets' at the bar beforehand, and just as I was about to walk out onto the tarmac, he rushed forwards with a show of emotion and affection. I didn't know what was happening. The incident was captured on camera; for years afterwards I always felt a rush of self-consciousness when I looked at the photo.

Like many grandmothers, though, Mum embraced her grandchildren with unconditional love. Consequently, the grandkids feel completely comfortable talking about anything, either with or in front of their grandma.

'I got the results of my pap smear,' one of them says.

'Oh yeah? How'd you go? Pass the potato salad, please,' another replies.

'Yeah, all good.'

'I'm getting a new tattoo,' another grandchild says. 'It's going to be an eagle with spread wings, and it'll have your name in the middle of it, Grandma.'

'What, you're getting "Grandma" tattooed on your arm?' says Mum.

'No – Diana! That's your name, isn't it!'

They all laugh.

'Well, the only thing I ask is that you spell it correctly.'

This reduces the grandchildren to hysterics.

The dinner goes off without a hitch. We cram around the table and everyone tucks heartily into the feast.

At some point the phones and cameras come out and the photos begin. In each one we place Mum in the middle, resplendent in her blue polyester fleece dressing gown, and we gather around her and take pictures. Someone starts to sing, and before we know it we're all belting out one of Mum's favourite call-and-response songs.

'I've got the joy, joy, joy, joy down in my heart!'

'Where?'

'Down in my heart!'

'Where?'

'Down in my heart!'

'I've got the joy, joy, joy, joy down in my heart, down in my heart to stay!'

Mum sings, claps and smiles, and the fact that she is part of a dinner party in her pyjamas and dressing gown is irrelevant. She is our queen bee and we are all happy to be, in this moment, buzzing and humming around her.

4

A TIGHT LITTLE UNIT

Tony

'Closed for winter,' reads the sign out the front of the pool.

'You're kidding,' I say to myself. Yes, there is an early-morning chill in the air but the sun is out and the mercury will rise to the mid-twenties today. This is not winter. A high of thirteen degrees and raining, that's winter. Plus, the pool's heated. I'd just got used to the soup-like twenty-nine degrees that the pool manager likes to keep the water temperature at, a good few degrees warmer than any pool in Melbourne. One time I asked him why he kept it so hot. 'No one will come if I don't,' he replied. I guess no one will come if the fucking pool's closed.

I'm a swimmer. Always have been. The story goes that before I was born my older siblings were promised a pool once the youngest could swim. After nine babies, I imagine doubt was growing that the pool would ever be built. Once it was clear that I was the last, a concerted effort was made to teach me to swim. Throughout the summer of 1964–65, I spent a lot of time at the Norwood pool in Adelaide, being coached by my very motivated siblings. It wasn't long before I was declared proficient and the digging commenced.

In more recent years I've become enamoured with open-water swimming, and have increasingly enjoyed (if that's the right word) swimming all year round, including through Melbourne winters in Port Phillip Bay. When Beck suggested we move to Mount Isa, I lamented that the nearest open water was the crocodile-infested mudflats and mangroves of the Gulf of Carpentaria, five hours to the north.

Until now, Beck and I had been making do with the pool. Despite the heat, it is underutilised and we often each have a lane to ourselves. The pool is on the western edge of town, adjacent to the mine, and as I swim down the lane each time I swing my head to take a breath I see the lead stack looming ominously overhead. In the evening, with the light of the setting sun refracted through the dust and fumes of the mine, it's quite beautiful, but it's hard not to imagine the toxic particles drifting down and landing on the surface of the pool. The official line is that the prevailing easterly winds blow the pollution to the west, away from the town. The theory goes that when the wind changes an alarm sounds and the smelter is shut down to prevent the lead blowing over town, but on some days as I race down the pool, sucking in the air, I can taste the fumes in the back of my mouth and wonder how diligent the mine managers are.

I take a longing look at the smooth surface of the pool through the chain-wire fence before slouching back to the car. Before going home I decide to detour to Brumbies, the only non-supermarket bakery in town, and pick up a vienna loaf. I text my poet friend Terry to lament the lack of sourdough.

'All loaf, no vienna,' he replies.

I manage a smile but my mood plummets when I walk back into the house. Diana's sitting in her chair and I can instantly tell her mood is flat.

'The pool's closed,' I tell her.

'Is that right?'

There are lolly wrappers on the kitchen bench, along with empty plastic eye-dropper vials, and a tea cup with a used teabag stuck to the bottom next to the sink. Beck's out of town for work and it's just Diana and me for the week. I feel my irritation rising.

'I'm going to give the lake a go,' I tell Diana, picking up my keys and swimming gear again.

The 'lake' is actually a dam around fifteen kilometres out of town. Beck says they used to swim out there all the time as kids, but now it's mainly the domain of jet skis and people fishing. I've asked a few locals but haven't been able to get a read on whether you can swim there now or not. Some screw up their noses and talk of duck lice. Others mutter about crocodiles, though it's widely accepted that freshwater crocs – the kind that are harmless to humans – are the only ones that inhabit the lake. While driving out there, I recall something Beck's brother David told me on the phone a few weeks ago: 'You'd be crazy to swim there. I know plenty of dickheads who bring back salties from the gulf and release them into the lake.'

'Why would they do that?' I asked.

'For a laugh.'

I don't find the idea at all funny.

The place is almost deserted when I arrive, and I park next to the picnic area. Then I spot one man in his early sixties drying himself on the cement slab in front of the canoe shed.

'So it's okay to swim here?' I ask.

'Absolutely. I swim every week.'

He points to an island in the middle. 'Sometimes I swim out there, and then on to the one behind it, and I'm gone for hours.'

I don't doubt it. He looks in good shape – the term 'fit as a trout' suddenly makes sense. I eye the distant islands, and then a line of yellow buoys closer in. A couple of laps around the buoys will be more my style, I decide.

The man tells me the canoeists have cleared a path through the duckweed directly in front of the canoe shed. 'That's the best place to enter,' he says. 'And don't leave your towel or clothes next to the lake's edge, if you don't want to get infested with lice.'

I thank him and strip down to my bathers and walk to the water. It's brown and murky, and surprisingly cold. Leaving my thongs at the edge, I tentatively step out onto the rocks and mud, and steel myself as I ease into the water. The channel is narrow and the weed is just below the surface. I force myself to glide quickly over the top, holding myself as high as I can, barely breathing, until I'm in the clear. Then, relieved that I'm not already itching from lice, I swim towards the middle yellow buoy, a couple of hundred metres directly out from the shore.

Once there, I strike out to the left and pick up my pace. But I have an overwhelming sense of wanting to close my eyes and go to sleep. It's as if I'm not getting enough oxygen to the brain. I immediately think of Diana in her chair or at the kitchen table, when she vagues out and becomes listless, sometimes falling in and out of sleep without seeming to realise it. When I watch her I imagine that this is how she'll die. Slowly running out of oxygen and drifting off to a final sleep in her chair. It doesn't seem like such a bad way to go.

As I round the yellow buoy at the western end, my oxygen intake and expenditure reach equilibrium and I feel a boost of energy. Not unlike Diana on the days following her admission to hospital after her heart attack, perky after spending twenty-four hours on oxygen.

I sprint along the line of buoys to the other end. When I get there I remove my goggles and look around. There are a couple of fishing boats out near the island, and one person walking a dog along the shore, but apart from that the place is empty. Not that I would know anybody. Other than Beck's mum, nieces and their families, I hardly know anyone in town. I share an office with one other person over twenty years younger than me, and have very little cause to engage with other professionals in town. We don't have kids in school and so haven't buddied up with their friends' parents.

Nevertheless, I have made a few tentative forays into the community. Not long after moving here I was driving down East Street, past the tennis courts, when I noticed a sign advertising Monday-night social tennis. I love tennis. I grew up with a tennis court and have played all my life. Despite the fact that I'm a completely mediocre player, I decided to try it out. I was greeted by Brendan, the club president, and his twelve-year-old son, Matthew. No one else turned up. After waiting awkwardly for a while, Brendan suggested Matthew and I have a hit. I felt slightly embarrassed but Matthew seemed completely at ease. We played a set and I won. His heart wasn't in it, I suspect. It wasn't surprising that neither he nor I suggested a second set. The following week I fronted up again. Brendan was dutifully there but no one else showed – not even Matthew. That was the end of social tennis.

A couple of weeks later I decided to join a writing group that met monthly at the library. I had a faint hope I'd meet some like-minded people, and that one thing would lead to another and we'd all be having post-group drinks at the pub across the road. But country towns are full of shy people, and when the convenor dismissed us at six on the dot everyone scurried out the door.

Despite this, I like the writing group. One of the things I knew Mount Isa would offer me was the time and solitude to write. I'm by nature a gregarious person, and have to force upon myself the discipline required to write. I sometimes wonder if being the youngest of a large family has something to do with this. I have a fear of missing out. As a child I was unable to lie in bed if I heard someone else up and about. I would drag myself out of bed so as not to miss out on any of the action, even if the action was merely someone eating toast.

My older siblings have strong memories of me always hanging around. As teenagers, they'd be engrossed in lurid conversation with friends around the kitchen table or in the lounge room. After a while they'd look up and see me quietly perched on the kitchen bench or on the back of the couch, eavesdropping. The conversation would stop, and either they'd wander off, leaving me stranded, or I'd take the hint and slink away. Later, like a moth drawn to a flame, I'd find another possie from which to listen and observe.

But in Mount Isa, without the distractions and the FOMO, I'm carving out time to write. Mainly it's weekdays in the mornings between six and seven, before work. On the weekends I scrounge time in among the garage sales, the gardening and the house rearrangements that Beck insists upon.

'I thought the plan was to get rid of junk, not buy more,' I say in vain, trying to resist another circuit of the garage sales.

'Think of it as a social outing – a date even,' she says. 'And while we're out we'll stop by the nursery. Isn't that exciting?'

I groan. 'Why're we buying more plants? Once your mum dies we're out of here.'

'For the resale value. And who knows how long we'll be here for? Mum's looking sprightly, don't you reckon?'

I know this will lead to an afternoon of hole digging and planting. My day of writing lost. I tell Beck half the plants will die and it'll be a waste of time and money.

'We've no shortage of time,' she says. 'And stop being a tight-arse – we're not paying rent.'

On top of all of this, I have Beck and Diana. We are becoming a tight little unit. Even with her intermittent flatness and untidiness,

Diana is very easy to live with, and I feel very welcome and comfortable in her house. On our first weekend, as Diana was getting ready to go to church, Beck flippantly asked her to pray for us. 'Why would I do that?' she replied, quick as a flash. 'I'll sing a prayer of thanks that you're here.'

Diana is also very interested in my work. She's particularly fascinated by the large native title meetings that I run. Who comes to them? What are they hoping for? Sometimes our conversations focus on the high drama associated with these meetings – the fights between families; the inter-generational resentments played out in a new arena; the deals struck to keep the claim afloat; the invective thrown at me, the white lawyer, who for a time at these meetings becomes the embodiment of the dispossession and oppression by the colonists.

To my surprise, I don't encounter in Diana the pervasive antagonism towards my work and Aboriginal people that overlays many of my interactions in western Queensland. The conversations that go dead when I'm asked what I do. The scepticism towards native title. The belief that Aboriginal people get special treatment, and it's only a matter of time before they take the pastoralists' property.

Diana displays none of this. At times she displays ignorance, sometimes referring to an Aboriginal person as 'dark-skinned' or even 'coloured'. But this is said as a point of reference, not as denigration. She's interested in the individual, and she offers no judgement.

And Beck and I are becoming closer. We've always been good mates – we like each other's company and make each other laugh. We have that ease that comes when you know that neither of you is going to be a dick or embarrass you in front of your friends or colleagues. Beck lights up a room when she enters it, and being back in her childhood home in Mount Isa, with its limitless sun and sky, has brought her even more sparkle and joyfulness, which she has transported into Madang Street and into our lives.

'Aren't you pleased I brought you here to paradise, and now I'm abandoning you?' she teased as we drove to the airport yesterday morning, past the mine workshops and rail shunting yards.

'Are you telling me you're not coming back?'

Beck smiled and shrugged.

'Ah, I get it,' I continued. 'I stay and look after your mum on my own.'

I stop my daydreaming, pull my goggles back on and do two more laps of the buoys before getting out. I feel cleansed and less irritable, and relieved that I've found a place to swim. No lice and no crocodiles – at least, none that I'm aware of.

I dry myself and sit in the sun for a while. It's mid-morning now and the temperature is rising, but I can feel my body temperature falling and I start to shiver. This is known as 'the drop'. When you swim in cold water, the body protects itself by shutting down the circulation of blood from the extremities – the arms and legs – and attempts to keep the warmest blood close to your internal organs. When you get out of the cold water and are exposed to warmth, the circulatory system kicks back in and the colder blood in your arms and legs cycles back into your core, bringing your body temperature down. I get in the car and, despite the trapped heat of the sun through the windows, shiver all the way back into town.

On the edge of town I call into the First n' Last store. Without a doubt this is the saddest shop I have ever been into. It's a takeaway shop that doubles vaguely as a grocery store. The oil from the fryer always smells stale, half the shelves are empty, and what stock it does have is ridiculously overpriced. Usually my sole purchase is the local paper that comes out on Tuesdays, Thursday and Saturdays. It's good only for the crossword (and the garage sale listings).

Diana has had a shower by the time I get home and seems chipper. I put on a pot of coffee, open up the house and tidy up the detritus while waiting for it to brew. I plonk the paper onto the table. 'Let's do the crossword.'

Diana immediately climbs out of her chair and shuffles towards the table.

'One down, loosen, seven letters,' I say.

Without missing a beat, Diana answers: 'Release.'

5

DOWN IN THE DUMPS

Rebecca

My phone pings. I can see that it's a text from Tony:

> How about the new Japanese place after work for sushi and sake? 😊

I grin and pause to think about what to text back. I look through the louvres of my study to the front lawn. Half of it is bathed in afternoon sun, and a canopy of frangipani trees shades the other half.

I've been at my desk all day so it would be good to go out, but I had planned on doing some gardening. I have a number of seedlings in pots that need to be transplanted. I've been meaning to do it for a few weeks, and I suspect some of them have already died due to heat and neglect.

Along the side of the lawn is a row of pots with frangipani cuttings. I've been trying to propagate some new trees. Frangipanis are family favourites, and my plan is to establish enough new trees to be able to give everyone a thriving one as a gift. These cuttings don't appear to be doing very well either. There is no new growth and I recently noticed some slimy black fungus around the bottom of one of the stems. When I touched it I could feel the softness of rotten innards, a mush close to liquid.

I told Mum about it.

'That's never happened to my cuttings,' she said.

'How do you propagate them?' I asked.

'I just snap a branch off and stick it in the soil,' she said. 'I'm not a gardener like you, but mine never die.'

'I wonder if I'm overwatering them?'

'Maybe,' said Mum. 'They're tropical plants and in most climates go for periods of time without water.'

I think she's probably right but it's so hard not to overwater. It's only October and the midday temperature is already in the high thirties. I'm still adjusting to the climate, and to the amount of water that both people and plants need.

One of the few luxuries that Mum has acquired over the last few years is a filtered water dispenser. Initially I scoffed and said I would only drink water out of the tap, but as it comes out at boiling point I have acquiesced to the cooler.

I do wonder how filtered the water really is. When I go to the shop to buy our fifteen-litre bottles I can't help but think about one of my favourite scenes in the movie *Slumdog Millionaire*. A young waiter in an Indian restaurant fills up an old plastic bottle with water from the tap, whacks a filter label on the bottle and then reglues the lid on.

I turn and look through the door of my study. I can see Mum slumped in her big green chair. The radio is on low but her eyes are shut. The glass of water I gave her an hour or so ago sits untouched on the side table.

Getting Mum to drink water is still a battle. I can't understand why she's not thirsty. I gulp down numerous glasses of water throughout the day, wake up in the middle of the night to drink more, and always wake up thirsty.

I often think about how little I drank as a kid. I'd have a big slurp from the water taps at school at lunchtime, and then another drink when I got home. If I was playing outside I might have a drink from the hose but that was about it. Sometimes we had water on the table at dinnertime but not all the time. I didn't ever drink water in the evenings or before bed. I don't remember feeling thirsty, but I did have a recurring dream about thirst as a kid.

I can still see and feel the dream: I am so thirsty and in front of me hovers a frosty glass of cold water. I stretch out and try to grasp the glass but it remains out of my reach. I stretch a bit more, and just as I almost grab it I wake up.

I told Tony about the dream.

'Sounds like you spent your childhood dehydrated,' he said.

I suspect he's right. I suspect we were all dehydrated. I don't remember anyone drinking nearly the amount of water that we drink now. No wonder there were so many fidgety and cranky kids at school.

I know that Mum's kidneys aren't working properly. She rarely goes to the toilet during the day, and most nights I massage her swollen legs and ankles. Her skin is dry, itchy and red. She scratches her legs and arms throughout the night until they bleed, so I'm constantly changing her sheets. I've been trying to get her to drink herbal tea rather than caffeinated tea but it's not going well.

We have the same conversation every day.

'Would you like a cup of tea, Mum?' I ask.

'What sort?' she asks.

'Herbal.'

I watch her do her disapproving nose twitch. 'Oh, all right.'

'You don't have to,' I say.

'Can I have normal tea?' she asks.

'How much water have you drunk today?' I ask.

'A few glasses.'

'When?'

'Are you the water monitor?' she asks.

'Yes,' I say. 'I am, actually!'

Mum gives a wry smile and I hand her a glass of water.

'Drink this,' I say, 'and then you can have a cup of normal tea.' I stand beside her and wait.

'Who are you now?' Mum asks. 'Nurse Ratched?'

I roll my eyes.

Mum drinks half of the glass of water and then I make her a cup of normal tea.

In many ways Mum is the ideal patient. She agrees with everything I suggest. The tension comes from the fact that she does not actually do the things she agrees to. If left unchecked she will stay immobilised in her chair all day, drink nothing and eat her way through a bag of lollies. When this happens, she becomes withdrawn and belligerent. I try all my tricks to engage her.

'Would you like to play a game of Upwords, Mum?'

'No,' she says.

'How about cribbage, then?'

'No.'

'What about we do a crossword? Or I could read you an article from the paper?'

Mum shakes her head.

'Are you okay, Mum?' I ask.

'I'm fine.'

'Would you like to sit outside for a bit?' I ask.

'No.'

'Are you annoyed with me, Mum?'

'I think I'll go and lie down in my room,' she says. With that, she gets up, goes to her room and shuts the door.

I don't know what to do when she's like this so I just let her be. On one level I think it's important to try to buck Mum up and get her out of her slump, but on another level I wonder what the point is. I know Mum thinks similarly. She recently told me that some mornings she wakes up, opens one eye and says out loud, 'You've got to be kidding!'

Even though this little anecdote made me laugh, I do wonder how keen Mum is on prolonging her life. And is her desire not to drink water all part of a larger plan to shut down? Is my desire to keep her healthy and engaged all about me? Am I the one who is too scared to let go?

A flutter of air outside causes a branch of frangipani to push up against the louvres. It's covered in flowers, and the sweet heady scent makes me think of long, cool drinks in a tropical garden. I text Tony back:

> I feel like sangria and tapas. How about we meet at the Spanish garden bar? 🌴 🍍 🍷

I smile to myself and press send. I stay at my desk and continue to look out the window. I love using this room as a study. I've always thought that it was the best room in the house. It has a view of the front garden, the street and the hill. It was another room that had been filled with junk for years.

Not long after we arrived, I said to Mum, 'We're going to clean the junk out of the front room so that I can have a study.'

'Junk is a pejorative word to describe the contents of that room,' she replied.

'How would you describe it?'

'A museum dedicated to uncatalogued and forgotten historical memorabilia.'

'Which is,' I said, 'a euphemism for junk.'

But Mum was right. When I started to clean the room out, I did find a myriad of uncatalogued and forgotten historical memorabilia. At the back of one cupboard was a coconut. I was so surprised that I took a photo and sent it to David. Quick as a flash he messaged back:

I brought that coconut back from a holiday on Magnetic Island in 1967. I wondered where it was! 😄

The cupboards, drawers and shelves were full of items that no one had looked at for years. I spent hours going through boxes of old sewing patterns and bags of fabric. Mum was an excellent dressmaker, and every pattern and remnant of fabric sparked a memory.

I found schoolbooks dating back to the 1950s, old clothes (including a couple of excellent 1970s body shirts that I added to my wardrobe), school uniforms that hadn't seen the light of day for over forty years, the dress Mum made me when I was confirmed in 1974, wilted Christmas decorations, dusty wrapping paper, unopened gifts, board games with missing parts, and bags stuffed full of letters dating back fifty years.

It took me days to pull everything out, and even longer to look at it all. This drove Tony spare. He wanted to get the whole lot into the skip and off to the dump.

'Every item in this room tells a story,' I told him.

'Well, hurry up and get to the end of the story!' he said.

The letters were the most difficult. I didn't have time to read them all, but I didn't want to throw them out either. What if there was a gem in there, like a letter that held the key to the secret in our family, and I'd thrown it out? Or even a letter that was significant historically?

Years ago, Mum had told me about a letter she received from her great-uncle when she was at boarding school.

'He told me about waving off Burke and Wills on their famous expedition,' she said.

'How old was he?' I asked.

'I think he was about six. It was in Melbourne in 1860. He told me about the camels, and how people lined the streets for miles to wave them off. He had a small flag.'

'Was he the Mission to Seafarers uncle?' I asked.

Mum thought about this. 'No. The Mission to Seafarers man was his dad, the Reverend Kerr Johnston,' she said.

Reverend Kerr Johnston was the family member who started the Victorian branch of the Mission to Seafarers. Years ago, Mum and I visited the building in Flinders Street and found a small plaque acknowledging Reverend Kerr Johnston's contribution. The building has a wonderful domed room, and I've always thought it would be a great place to do a show. Maybe one day, I think, I will write about my family's connection with this famous movement and building.

'What happened to the letter?' I asked Mum.

'I had it for years and eventually threw it out.'

'It must be the only thing you ever did throw away.'

Mum laughed, but it was also pretty close to the truth.

I didn't find the letter from my great-uncle but I did find all the letters I wrote to my parents when I was an exchange student in 1980. I read a few and then stopped; the self-absorbed nature of my adolescent writing was too uncomfortable.

I found letters that I sent when I first started at university. In one letter I described going for an agency visit to the rape crisis centre in Brisbane, 'Women's House'.

'The organisation is managed by a group of very butch looking ladies,' I wrote at the time. I nearly passed out with both embarrassment and laughter when I read that. Little did I know that within a few years I would become a lifelong feminist, work at Women's House, live as the 'token hetero' in a lesbian share house, and drop the phrase 'ladies and gentlemen' from my vocabulary for ever.

My favourite find was the hundreds of old bank statements dating back to the 1980s. These were stacked in piles based on date and year, and bound with either string or rubber bands. Mum's attention to detail, amid what could honestly be described as chaos, was impressive.

'Why have you kept all these?' I asked her.

'The Australia Taxation Office recommends that people hold on to their financial items for at least seven years after lodging a tax return.'

'But you're a pensioner – you haven't needed to lodge a tax return for years.'

'Well, the ATO might send me a letter requesting evidence of my financial situation.'

'Mum, I suspect you are of less interest to the ATO than anyone else in the country!'

This became a running joke. If an unknown car pulled up in front of the house and Mum asked, 'Who's that?', I would tell her it was the ATO. 'They want to know if you really did donate $50 to the Guide Dog Association in 2001 or if it was actually $45.'

'Oh, do shut up, Rebecca!'

The problem is, like Mum, I find it terribly hard to throw anything out. Instead of sorting through things, I spend whole afternoons photographing items and texting the family with evidence of their forgotten 'treasures'. What starts out as a chore becomes an afternoon of deep connection.

I end up doing what I swore I wouldn't: packing boxes and suitcases of 'precious' items and placing them under the house for later sorting and distribution. I know what I'm doing is crazy, and I'm reminded of something Dad used to say about leftovers after a meal: *Should we throw these out tonight or put them in the fridge and throw them out next week?*

The frangipani trees provide good cover so I can sit and watch the comings and goings of the street pretty much undetected.

Sometimes I feel like Dad. He liked to sit in the lounge chair closest to the front door so that he could have a 'stickybeak' on the action of the street. It feels like hours since I saw Shawn, the young man who lives across the road, come home on the community school bus. Most mornings and afternoons I either hear or see the old diesel Coaster cruise around the corner and pull up across the street.

Shawn is a charming young man who has grown up faster than most. At just sixteen years old, he lives with his partner, Cheyenne, their eight-month-old baby, Jaydon, and their dog, Maleka.

I have a love/hate relationship with Maleka. She's a small, stocky black dog of ill-defined breed, and spends most of her time lying in the middle of the street. She barks at and chases kids going past on bikes, and growls and sneers at everyone else. Every day I watch terrified kids, runners, people with prams and the postie try to fend her off. She is pint-sized but looks like she'd serve up a distemper-laced bite. Shawn and Cheyenne stand on their verandah and, at the top of their voices, scream, 'Shut up, Maleka!' They never come down and pull her away.

I'm not a natural with dogs but I have started to take Maleka on. It's almost like sport. When I see kids looking terrified on their bikes, I rush out and scream, 'Shut up, Maleka!' Then I tell the kids, 'Don't worry about her – her bark is worse than her bite. Just scream at her – everyone else does!'

When I come up the hill in my car and see Maleka lying in the middle of the street, I mutter under my breath, 'Fucking Maleka!' I drive as close as I can towards her before swerving. Maleka never moves, and we give each other steely glares. Some days I wonder what is happening to me. I have never harmed an animal, and this new desire to scare her is alarming.

Shawn told Tony that when he and Cheyenne first got together (he was thirteen and she was eighteen) he knew it was time to 'step up'. When we were thirteen, Tony and I both agree, we were a long way from 'stepping up'.

For months before we met Shawn and Cheyenne we thought they were engaged in some form of nefarious activity. People and cars would come and go from the house at all times of the day and night. Often a car would pull up and beep the horn, someone would saunter out from the house for a quick word through the window, then the car would screech off again.

We heard a variety of negative but unsubstantiated stories about the occupants. Though we both tried, neither Tony nor I could catch anyone's eye from the house. But then one afternoon when I was gardening, Shawn walked past and I called out to him, 'Hey!'

Shawn stopped and looked at me. 'Hey,' he replied.

'My name's Beck,' I said. 'My husband, Tony, and I live in this house now with my mum.'

Shawn wandered over to the fence. 'I'm Shawn,' he said, and

we shook hands. 'Yeah, I seen youse here doing the garden. It looks real good.'

'Thanks,' I said. 'Lot of work.'

'We're gunna get some topsoil and do our place,' he told me.

I looked across the road to their house and the dust bowl that was the front yard. It was going to need a bit more than some topsoil, I thought.

'How's the baby?' I asked.

'Jaydon,' said Shawn. 'He's great – real cheeky little bubba but we love him.'

'That's so good,' I said, smiling.

We've been mates ever since. We mainly talk at the fence but sometimes he and Cheyenne come in and bring Jaydon so Mum can see him. Although this young couple have lived opposite her house for a couple of years, Mum only met them after Tony and I moved in. Now she enquires regularly about them, as they do about her.

Lately things seem to have improved for Shawn and Cheyenne. The amount of drive-by traffic has fallen, and Shawn seems to make it onto the school bus every morning. He recently told me that Cheyenne is expecting another baby, and how happy he is.

From the shadows across the front lawn I guess that it's probably about five o'clock. I should get up from my desk and go and check on Mum. Other than a short break at lunchtime I have been at my desk all day and have given her no attention. As far as I know, she hasn't moved from her chair.

Today has been a home day, but Mum is often out and about. To keep on top of her various outings, we spend Sunday nights going through her week. I write appointments and activities on the wall calendar and into my diary.

'Monday?' I'll ask.

'I'm having coffee tomorrow with Beryl at ten am at the Buffs Club.'

'Do you want me to drive you?'

'No, Beryl will pick me up.'

Beryl is Mum's good friend. She's much younger and treats Mum with great respect. They met at Legacy. I often say to Beryl how lucky Mum is to have her as a friend, but she always says, 'I'm the lucky one!'

'And Tuesday?' I ask.

'I think we have an appointment with the cardiologist,' says Mum. 'Check the letter that I stuck on the calendar.'

I find the letter clasped onto the calendar with a peg. There are many bits of paper stuck to things with pegs in this house. Mum has one of those old-fashioned wall letter racks, but apart from a few lolly wrappers it remains empty. Mum likes peg filing.

'Yes,' I say. 'Cardiologist at three pm on Tuesday.'

'You'll take me to that?' asks Mum.

'Yes,' I say.

'Wednesday: shopping,' says Mum.

'Is there a Legacy lunch this Wednesday?' I ask.

'No, that'll be next week.'

'Thursday: hairdresser,' I say. This is a standing appointment: every Thursday Mum gets her hair set. 'And Friday: the home?'

Mum nods. Every second Friday Mum goes with Marlene, another volunteer from her church, to give a service at the aged care facility.

'Anything else?' I ask. 'Mothers' Union meeting? Lunches, morning coffees?'

'Church on Sunday,' says Mum.

'Yep, got that.'

Mum has a lot of medical appointments. She sees her GP, an

ophthalmologist and a cardiologist. I go to all the appointments with her. Everyone is always running late so we spend a lot of time in waiting rooms. We do magazine puzzles, and if there's no reading material we make up games.

I say to Mum, 'C G E E R E M Y N.'

'Say the letters again,' she replies.

'C G E E R E MY N.'

'Men,' says Mum.

I nod.

'Mere.'

I nod.

'Mean.'

'There's no A,' I say.

'Germ,' says Mum.

'Good one!'

'Say the letters again.'

'C G E E R E MY N,' I repeat.

Mum writes the letters in the air with her finger as I say them. She thinks for a moment. 'Emergency!'

'Good one, Mum!'

Mum gives me the thumbs-up.

Mum is intelligent and capable, but when I'm in the consultation rooms with her I realise that she has lost her confidence.

The medical staff are gentle and thorough, but with each visit Mum leaves me to ask more of the questions. The doctors pick up on this and start to talk directly to me. I try to divert back to Mum.

'How often does your mother feel dizzy?' asks Mum's cardiologist, Dr Mascot.

I turn to Mum and ask, 'How often do you feel dizzy, Mum?'

Mum looks directly at me and starts to speak. I turn and look at Dr Mascot so that Mum will focus her answer on him too and not me. Sometimes it works and sometimes it doesn't.

I wonder what would happen if I wasn't here.

Mum and I are driving down Camooweal Street. We're heading home from the hospital and discussing Dr Mascot.

'How old do you think he is?' asks Mum.

'Twelve,' I reply.

Mum laughs. 'I think he's about twenty-eight.'

'You think everyone is about twenty-eight, Mum.'

'How old do you really think he is?' she asks, laughing.

'Thirty-five,' I reply.

'I like the little bow he gives when he meets us,' says Mum.

'And the hand behind the back when he does it,' I say.

'Like a waiter.'

We both smile.

'Let's take the script for the new medication to the chemist now,' I say.

'Okay,' says Mum.

Dr Mascot has increased the dosage of Mum's medicine: he feels her blood pressure is still too low. This is the second change since I've been here.

We park opposite the chemist and Mum opens her purse.

'You're right, Mum,' I say. 'I'll get this.'

Mum hands me fifty dollars. 'Okay, you get the medication, but I need a new pair of compression stockings.'

When I get back into the car with Mum's medication and her new stockings, I hand her the change. It's only a few coins.

As I'm putting on my seatbelt, Mum says, 'I was thinking, when you were in the chemist, what will happen to me when you go back to Melbourne to live?'

I stop what I'm doing and sit back in my seat. 'We're not going back to Melbourne, Mum.'

'But you said you would only stay for a year.'

'No, we'll stay until … you know.'

'The end?'

'Yeah, the end.'

'When did you decide this?' asks Mum.

'On about day one! But we only agreed to it more formally over the last few months.'

'Why didn't you tell me?'

I think about this. 'I thought it was obvious from our actions,' I say.

Mum nods. 'Yes, it has been, but it's good to hear you say it.'

I nod.

Mum touches my hand and says, 'Thank you.' She looks at the change that I've given her and says, 'Let's go to McDonald's for an ice cream.'

Though I despise everything about this food outlet, we head for the drive-through and buy two soft-serve cones. Such is life.

It's Thursday night. Tomorrow Mum goes with Marlene to the aged care facility to administer a church service.

Mum tells me that most of the people who come to the service are not actually Anglicans; in fact, she suspects that most of them have very little interest in Christianity at all. She assumes, and probably rightly so, that most of the people who come are more interested in the morning tea she and Marlene provide. I sit at the table and watch Mum as she prepares her food.

When Mum first started going to 'the home', as she calls it, she would bake biscuits or a cake. Now, however, there are strict health and safety rules in place, and you can only take packaged food into the facility.

Mum and Marlene have a pretty good arrangement worked out. Mum buys cheese and biscuits, and Marlene buys doughnut balls from the plaza. Mum opens the packet of pre-sliced cheese and takes out each slice. She then unwraps each slice from the plastic, cuts it into biscuit-size pieces and puts them in a Tupperware container. She opens the packet of biscuits, takes them out of their wrapper and puts them into another plastic container.

'Are you allowed to do that?' I ask.

'What?'

'Open the packets and handle the food? Doesn't that defeat the purpose of the policy?'

'No one has ever said anything,' Mum says.

I watch as she continues cutting the cheese and ask no more questions. When she's finished, Mum places the two containers in the front of the fridge so it'll be easy for her to find them in the morning.

One time she accidentally took a plastic container out of the fridge that had leftover mashed potato in it, and took that instead of the cheese. Apparently the residents were in hysterics over this, but some still chose to have the mash on their biscuits.

My phone pings; it's Tony.

> Change of plan. Some of the gang from work have invited us to join them at the vodka bar for drinks and blinis. You in?

I smile and text back:
> Sounds beaut! If you get there first, order me a martini. 🍸 ♥ 😲

I look out from my desk to the lounge room; Mum is still asleep in her chair. I think about waking her up. I struggle with the fact that, in the bigger scheme of things, surely it's not a big deal if she spends her day inside the house in a somnolent blur. She doesn't demand anything or express any discomfort or unhappiness.

The issue, however, is that when she spends her days like this, both her mood and energy slump to such a degree that by the end of the day flatness takes a grip upon her that's difficult to budge. It's a small house, and if left unchecked, Mum's grey mood can dominate. If I wake Mum, I will have to engage with her, otherwise she will remain flat and the evening will be unpleasant for her – and for us.

But I don't feel like engaging today. I feel a bit flat myself, and I know why. Like Mum, I've been sitting for too long, and it's been a long week of working alone. I need more stimulation and company. I'm pretty self-contained and adore Mum, but I know this week has been a bit too much of just the two of us. I see the change that happens in Mum after her outings. She is always far more upbeat. It's probably the same for me; other than going to the shops and Mum's appointments, I have very few outings.

I feel envious of Tony. His job puts him in contact with all sorts of people. Every day he has a new story about someone he's met with or spoken to on the phone. I don't want a lot. My life is pretty full. My Melbourne projects are keeping me very busy, and likewise my life with Mum, Tony and our extended Mount Isa family.

I'm good at working alone but I love working with other people. I like a balance between time alone and time with others, and at the moment things are weighted too heavily to the former. I need to find a small contract or some part-time work so that I can mix up my lifestyle a bit more. So far the only paid employment I've been able to secure was teaching a few aqua aerobics sessions at the local pool. But I'm not going to the pool at the moment as I've had a falling-out with the pool manager.

Actually, that's not entirely true. I'm fine, but the manager has fallen out with me.

It surprised me because I thought we were getting on quite well. I wouldn't have said we were boon companions, but he had employed me to do a few classes. No one would call him sanguine; in most of my dealings with him I found him to be offhand and borderline unfriendly. But I felt I was just starting to break through his tight veneer and get the occasional smile and hello.

This all changed a few weeks ago. 'Your music is too slow,' he told me. In the rarefied world of aqua aerobics, this is akin to a sin. The music needs to be at a certain number of beats per minute in order to match the required cardio workout.

'What?' I said.

'Some of the women have complained.'

This was news to me. The feedback I'd received from the class had been to the contrary. 'My music is industry standard,' I told him confidently.

And with that he stopped employing me. Oh, the fickle world of aqua aerobics!

So here I am with all my fancy-pants university degrees and qualifications, but no bastard wants to employ me! It's so sad that it's actually funny.

But I can't complain. In a few weeks I'll be heading off to Melbourne again for three weeks. After a fairly torturous few months of work, I have finally finished the treatment documents for the film. My inexperience as a film writer has made it a long and hard task.

When I'm in Melbourne, *HERE* will open and I'll do my development and showing of *Resting Bitch Face*. My play *I'll Be There* with the Victorian Trade Union Choir will also have a number of shows on, and I have been engaged again as the director. We'll also celebrate Lucille's twenty-first birthday, so there's a lot to look forward to.

Knowing all this makes my current lethargy feel all the more self-indulgent. I chose to be here – no one asked me to come, and no one expected me to come – so really I just have to 'step up' and get on with it.

Nonetheless, my lack of stable income and employment keeps me awake at night. I'm in my early fifties, don't have a secure job, don't own a house, have a second-hand car and am back living with my mother in a town where no one knows me, and where no one seems particularly interested in my skills.

We're still paying rent on our place in Melbourne, and my lack of income means I am dependent on Tony. I have never earned a lot of money but, other than when our children were really small, I've always been able to bring in enough to pay my own way.

Mum is very generous and often wants to pay for the household's groceries and living expenses, but Tony and I insist on going halves. I'm an expert at eking out an excellent existence on a meagre amount of money, but currently it feels very close to the bone.

I get into a conversation with a young professional at choir. I tell her how difficult it has been for me to make connections with people through my work. 'I email people and ring them, but no one ever gets back to me,' I say.

'Everyone is so busy,' she says.

'Yeah,' I say.

'Once you get something here, it just takes off,' she says. She tells me about the fast-tracking that occurred with her career once she came to Mount Isa.

'My problem,' I say, 'is that no one here knows my work, so I have no one to champion me.'

'I champion myself,' she says.

'Oh, I do too,' I say, 'but how I network and connect with people is very similar to the way I work with people. I need a point of entry, and if that isn't there then I'm not good at talking myself up. That's not how I work.'

'It's all about self-belief,' she says, and moves on.

'Yeah, thanks for that,' I mutter to myself.

I start to wonder if what I am looking for doesn't exist. Am I naive – or, worse, selfish? I want a job that allows me to look after Mum, that has the flexibility so that I can return to Melbourne for my project work, that brings me into contact with like-minded people who value my talents, and that pays decent money. Does such a job even exist?

I've spent years getting my kids through school, and supporting Tony through a postgrad law degree and two federal elections where he ran for the House of Representatives with the Australian Greens. And he has spent years supporting my arts practice. We thought we were living the dream, investing in a lifestyle that would eventually reap some rewards. But now, as I sit at this desk, I wonder where it's all going to lead.

Sometimes I feel anger towards Mum and the rest of my family for not discussing this situation. Why didn't we talk about this? Why didn't we make plans for Mum and her old age? Why didn't we put things in place years ago? We are a family of avoiders. I suspect that if things had gone on as they were, Mum would have been forced into the aged care facility and that would have been that. And without doubt she would have been miserable in there.

I know that I need to get Mum up and out of her chair, and engaged in a game of Upwords or a crossword puzzle – or, better still, take her outside for some fresh air and exercise. Getting her out of her chair also means I can give it a quick clean. When she spends all day in the big vinyl chair, the whole house starts to smell slightly sour. Many years ago she famously said that she 'loathed exercise', but I know that getting her moving will stimulate some endorphins and improve her mood.

The truth is there are no Japanese restaurants or Spanish bars in Mount Isa, and nor is there a vodka bar. We've never had an invitation from 'the gang' at Tony's work to join them for Friday drinks as there is no gang. He works with just one other person, a lovely woman who is much younger than us, and who is keen to get home after work to her fella and their baby.

Tony and I do the texting routine each Friday because it makes us smile and keeps at bay the nagging feeling that we are missing out on a more exciting life back in the big smoke. Who knows? Perhaps if we were back in Melbourne, we'd be having the same text messaging sequence but without the irony. That doesn't sound like nearly as much fun! I text Tony:

Hey, how about we just have quiet one at home?

He replies immediately:
That sounds perfect. I'll go to the bottle shop and get some beers and a bottle of wine.

I write back:
And some of those new gourmet chips … Mum loves them! ☺

We both know I'm the one who loves chips the most.

From my window I can hear Shawn, Cheyenne and baby Jaydon talking and laughing as they head to the park with Maleka. I'm tempted to call out to them, but I don't want to interrupt this moment in which they look so happy and content.

I go to my room and put on my new pineapple muu-muu that my friend Beverly has made and sent to me. It is bright green with large brown, yellow and green pineapples on it. It screams 'relaxation'! I run a comb through my hair, wash my face, and put on a bit of lippy and a pair of shiny earrings. I walk to the lounge and gently wake Mum.

'Where are you going?' she asks.

'Here,' I say.

'Here?'

'Yes. We're having drinks when Tony gets home.'

Mum nods and smiles. She gets up and shuffles to her room. I hear doors opening and shutting and the tap being turned on and off. After a short time Mum comes back into the lounge wearing a fresh muu-muu. She too has washed her face and combed her hair. We smile at each other and head outside.

I lead Mum around the backyard and we look at all the new plants Tony and I have put in. Lots of the native bushes are in bloom. Mum gets very close so that she can see them. 'The lorikeets and rosellas will love these,' she says.

I take her down to the back of the garden and show her the pineapple and aloe vera plants I'm putting in.

'Are you planning on planting out the whole backyard with pineapples?' she asks.

'Maybe,' I say.

'They're bromeliads, aren't they?' she asks.

'Yes,' I say.

We walk around to the front and she looks at my frangipani cuttings in the pots. 'Put them in the full sun for a few days,' she says. 'It might dry them out.'

While she does her stepping exercises up and down the front steps, I move the pots into the sunshine.

When Tony gets home, he brings drinks and chips out to the verandah. Mum and I sit and watch him water the garden. Soon we'll cook dinner together. Fish and salad has become our Friday-night specialty. Tony has picked up fresh barramundi, caught in the Gulf of Carpentaria and sent down to the fish shop at the ice works. Mum has said she'll make the salad. She is bright and chirpy.

After dinner we might sit on the verandah and listen to music, or maybe we'll play a game of Upwords. Tomorrow is Saturday, and I think about going to a garage sale or having a spin around Kmart. There are so many possibilities ahead.

6

TABLES TURNED

Tony

Bernice picks me up at 8 am to take me to the hospital for my hernia operation. A couple of snips in my abdomen, poke the intestine back through the abdominal muscle, stitch me back up and I'll be done.

'I should be right for the board meeting at six this evening,' I tell her. 'I'll text you when I'm done and you can pick me up.'

This meeting with one of the native title groups has taken months to organise, and I'm adamant that it should go ahead, and that I should be there.

'We'll see,' says Bernice.

I nod to the young Aboriginal man in his pyjamas smoking near the entrance. He has a patch over one eye, and is trailing a drip trolley. He gives me a smile.

I got the hernia six weeks ago, just before a bushwalking trip on Hinchinbrook Island with members of my family. I wasn't going to pull out – the trip had been six months in the making. Despite getting clearance from my doctor, and some anti-constipation drugs – 'Avoid straining at all costs,' he warned – I spent the five days hiking down the eastern flank of the island in perpetual fear of my abdominal muscle locking off around my lower intestine, which would result in me being airlifted off the island.

But my fear was mild in comparison to my friend Brad's. After my daughter Lucille realised she couldn't come on the trip, I offered the vacancy to Brad. 'You'll be the only non-Kelly,' I told him. He took up the offer regardless.

Brad had recently been diagnosed with melanoma, and was keen to walk the island again while he still could. It wasn't until we were well into the hike that I understood how unwell Brad was. Normally he would be up front blazing the trail, exploring side routes and skylarking around. On this trip he hung well back, often bringing up the rear. He never gave up but I knew he was struggling. At nights he tossed and turned in a lather of sweat as his heavy-duty medication coursed through his veins, and would wake up agitated and drained.

I was also worried about my oldest brother, Martin. He had not long ago recovered from a heart attack, and was susceptible to atrial fibrillation. He too had been given the all-clear by his doctor, but on the long, hot walk up from Zoe Bay, Martin alerted us to the fact that he was 'in AF'. I had a satellite phone at the top of my pack and made sure I was close to him as we plodded slowly up the spur. That was the last big day of walking, and it was with enormous relief that we made camp in good health that night.

Despite these medical anxieties, the trip was amazing and I felt extremely lucky that I had the opportunity to do it. Beck had wanted to come but couldn't. When making the decision to come to Mount Isa, one of the things in our 'plus' column was the promise of lots of weekends away together – trips out bush with the swag, sorties to the gulf and the like. But the reality had been much different. Diana tried respite once and didn't like it, and she wasn't keen to go back, insisting that she was fine to look after herself. Beck concluded that we could leave Diana home alone for a couple of days but no more, and only if the nieces were able to call in daily.

On the way to Hinchinbrook, I had had the opportunity to see my brother Paul and nephew Dan play at a drought-relief concert organised by my cousin. Beck was able to slip away for two nights and join me.

We drove through Kynuna, in the Channel Country south of Cloncurry. It was here in 1991, stranded in floods for five days and camping on the floor of some old shearers' quarters, that we had decided to get married. The shearers' quarters were still standing, but only just. They were extremely dilapidated and stood forlorn, surrounded by a falling-down rusty fence, red dirt and weeds. Surprisingly, there was a 'For sale' sign hanging off the fence, creaking in the breeze. Beck posted a picture on Facebook with the tagline: 'In this building we decided to get married over 30 years ago. Now we are going to buy it, do it up and move here. Full circle.' It wasn't meant to be taken seriously, and most people who know us would know that we're not the 'doing up' type. Our idea of renovating is plonking an old caravan in the backyard and running out an extension lead from the laundry, which is what we did when Beck's nephew Brian came to live with us in Daylesford fifteen years earlier. Within minutes, though, Beck's phone was lighting up with congratulatory posts: 'Awesome! ... Great news! ... Go Beck and Tone!' There were some alarmed ones too: 'Are you kidding? Don't do it!'

We arrived in Longreach well in time for the concert, which was to take place on the grass outside the Hall of Fame. The show, which included support from Troy Cassar-Daley, was fantastic. My sister Anne was there as well, and our cousin and his family and friends treated us like royalty – until I mentioned my work.

'So you're Paul's brother?' one fella in moleskins, a Wrangler shirt and R.M.Williams boots asked backstage.

'Yep,' I replied.

Another in an almost identical outfit chimed in: 'Have you come up from Melbourne too?'

'No, I live in Mount Isa.'

They both nodded encouragingly. I was almost a local.

'What work do you do?' The first one again.

'I work in native title.'

Silence. The men shuffled uncomfortably.

'Mainly with the people around Mount Isa,' I continued, 'but also with the Winton traditional owners just down the road here.' I didn't know how to stop. 'The claim is only over Crown land, you know, but that does include pastoral leases. But don't worry, pastoralists' rights will always trump native title rights.'

My nephew Dan, who had overheard the conversation, came to rescue me. 'Another beer, Tone?'

'Yes, please.' I looked at the men. 'You fellas need a drink?'

They shook their heads. Saying our farewells, Dan and I walked off together. 'Perhaps stick to the State of Origin or the weather,' Dan advised.

He was right: the scions of the early settlers – the great-grandchildren of the murderers, dispersers and dispossessors – clearly didn't want to bat the breeze about native title.

At the hospital I sign in at the day surgery reception desk, and the young woman on duty directs me to a foyer on level one, where I am to wait until called by the nurse. There are four other people ahead of me, so I suspect I'm in for a long wait. I send Beck a text:

About to go under the knife. How are you?

She replies:
All good. I feel bad. I should be there with you.

I don't mind that Beck's not here. She has a play on in Melbourne, and these trips out of Mount Isa are essential so she can maintain her career. I'm surprised at how difficult she's found it to get a foot in the door here, given how skilled and experienced she is. But she's been away for thirty-five years, and that makes her an outsider. The fact that she's now based in Melbourne – the big city – doesn't help. I'm lucky I have a workplace to go to each day, whereas Beck sits at her desk in the study only a couple of metres away from Diana, day in and day out.

I text:
I'm fine. How's Melbourne? How did the show go last night?

Beck replies:
Really good. The audience seemed to like it.

I am fine, I realise. The trips to Longreach and then Hinchinbrook have restored my sense of balance. The previous few months, I have to admit, had been hard work.

In August Rebecca was away for three weekends in a row. On the first weekend was the Mount Isa rodeo. I was excited to go and had planned to spend the evening with Belinda, Seppo and their daughters. But one of the girls was sick so Belinda wasn't able to come. I arrived early to see the parade, which (rather bizarrely) is called the Mardi Gras Parade. There was neither bling nor razzle-dazzle, just a few trucks with kids on the back, waving and throwing glitter and lollies into the crowd.

I thought Seppo would text me when he arrived, but he didn't and, feeling shy, I chose not to contact him. After the parade I went into the arena and watched a few events. The bull riding is the most popular, with contenders attempting to stay on a bucking bull for eight seconds. That doesn't sound long, but on a wildly bucking and kicking bull it is, and many riders don't make it. I found it an anticlimactic sport, with lots of time spent waiting around. After the bull riding I stayed on for the 'rope and tie'. This involves someone on horseback chasing down a startled calf with a lasso, jumping on top of it and immobilising it by tying up its feet. I was fascinated and appalled at the same time.

From the arena I went to sideshow alley and stood behind the gathering crowd at Fred Brophy's boxing tent. He was banging the drum and spruiking for local wannabes to take on his boxers, and for punters to pay the entry fee and watch the fights. So this is what 'rallying around the drum' actually means, I realised. Despite Fred's hype, I couldn't shift my forlorn mood, and went home.

The next weekend my mood fell even further. It came out of the blue. I'm by nature buoyant and rarely feel anything worse than a mild torpor, but not that day. I went into town on Saturday morning to buy some groceries and look for some heat beads to blind-bake some pastry. Diana and I planned to cook meat pies together: me preparing the pastry, she the filling.

It was the radio interview I heard with a permaculture hunt-and-gather man from the Central Highlands of Victoria that did me in. He could even have been someone I knew from when I lived in that part of Victoria years ago. I certainly knew his kind: people who live with a small footprint, wholesome and rugged, with skills to build high-tech, low-energy houses from timber sourced from their own block, and who can grow mountains of organic food, which they then pickle and preserve, and who rear, butcher, smoke and cure their own livestock.

The man on the radio described taking his home-schooled kids out into the forest to hunt for their dinner using a bow and arrow. I could picture him and his kids walking through the dripping woodlands. I could taste the moisture in the air. I could feel the dark, friable soil in my hands, from which plump vegetables would be plucked. I could smell the sourdough baking in the woodstove, and hear the glug of the dark ale and the gentle murmur of companionship.

I looked out into the glare of Miles Street, with its ugly iron-clad shops. The huge pub on the corner full of pokies, oversized steaks and mass-produced beers held nothing for me. I recognised none of the sun-damaged, tight-lipped people clambering out of their oversized four-wheel drives. I was a stranger in this alien land. The long weekend stretched before me. My only outing apart from this was likely to be taking Diana to church on Sunday morning.

An overwhelming sense of despair descended on me like a pall. I sat in the car, immobilised, with tears welling in my eyes. I was tired of the harshness of the town. Tired of its sameness. The mind-numbing conventionality. I was tired of the fucking ugliness.

My sister Mary Jo once said, when she moved to Brisbane from Melbourne forty years ago, that 'Queenslanders as a race are uglier than Victorians'. It was an outrageous thing to say on the face of it, but her observation was twofold. Firstly, at that time in Brisbane there was very little ethnic diversity, and most people were of Anglo-Celtic stock. Not the most attractive genetic pool, let's face it. (I feel free to say that, being 75 per cent Anglo-Celtic.) Secondly, there was a lack of interest in fashion and grooming, which was rooted in an anti-intellectual, anti-cultural, take-me-as-you-find-me attitude, which seemed to deepen the further north and west you went.

Looking out of my car window at the red-faced people walking down Miles Street wearing branded T-shirts, long shorts and thongs, my despair deepened. I'm not a particularly snappy dresser, and I'm partial to T-shirts (without a logo, mind you), shorts (though not long) and thongs myself, but right then I craved some difference. I wanted to see someone with a sense of style walk past. I wanted my eyes to rest upon something different, something with softness and grace.

The night before, the barking dogs had been particularly bad, and the lack of sleep wasn't helping my mood. This town is full of dogs that bark. Big, ugly mongrel dogs that pace and seethe in the confines of their heavily fenced yards. Every one of our immediate neighbours has one or more dogs, and they all bark incessantly. I have no idea what sets them off, but once one starts they all go and the sound reverberates around the rocky hills. It has become one of our favourite topics of conversation. Diana's not generally up for much chatting in the morning, but nevertheless most days we discuss the dogs. 'Did you hear the dogs last night?' I ask.

'Yes, they were bad,' Diana replies.

'I hardly slept,' I add.

'I rarely sleep,' Diana concludes.

No one ever seems to walk the dogs. No wonder they bark. My great-niece's boyfriend, Travis, told me that many dogs are kept for pigging – or, as he says, *piggin'*. Travis himself likes to go piggin' – and campin' and fishin', for that matter. I now understand the cages on the back of utes I see around town. 'They're for cartin' the dogs when you go piggin',' he said.

Travis also educated me about *boxin'*. 'Once them dogs have cornered the pig, you slit its throat and throw it on the back of the ute. Then drop it in the box back in town.'

The box, I discovered, is an air-conditioned container that, when it's full of dead pigs, gets transported to the pet food factory. Mount Isa dogs are not for promenading.

I knew that my despair wasn't being brought on just by the

harshness of the town or my lack of sleep – it was born of something deeper, something that had been brewing since we came to Mount Isa. Rebecca and I haven't accumulated much wealth. We have some money in a term deposit from the sale of a house we once owned in Daylesford, but it isn't much. I have a reasonable super balance but Beck, as a consequence of being a self-employed artist for most of her professional life, has virtually none. Age is creeping up on us – although that seems a ridiculous thing to think about when you're living with a ninety-year-old – and we're starting to worry about being poor in retirement.

Health permitting, we have only fifteen or so good earning years ahead of us. For many years I've assumed we had plenty of time to sort out our retirement, but now the future feels as if it's on our doorstep. Some people buy lotto tickets; we've gambled on some unforeseen event putting us in clover. An extremely well-paying job? My short-lived career as a Collins Street lawyer was my best chance of that. A cascade of royalties from Beck's writing? Perhaps that's still to come. As we're ageing, we're becoming more and more aware that dreams are not the foundation upon which to build financial security.

I rail against this preoccupation and feel that it's a middle-class obsession. An indulgence. But that's wrong: all people, regardless of class, are concerned about their old age. Security is a universal striving. I try to reassure myself that in Australia, come what may, with our meagre savings and super, combined with the pension and other social support services, we'll be able to keep ourselves. We'll definitely be better off than the vast majority of people in the world. It will be a small and simple life, and different to that lived by many of our peers, who have kept their eye on the long game. We won't have the beautifully renovated inner-city house. We won't have the overseas trips. We will have to be discerning about the food and clothes we buy and the things we do. In my

114

worst moments I imagine us rattling around a cold and rundown house, wearing ill-fitting op-shop jeans, waiting for our children to visit. In the early hours of the morning, as I lie in bed with my eyes wide open, it's shame and fear that churns my stomach.

I turned the radio off and got out of the car. The permaculture man's puritanism was starting to get to me. No doubt inherited wealth was what gave him the luxury to get off the grid! I went into Bella Duck, a homewares shop. I like Bella Duck, it's well stocked with good-quality kitchenware. An oasis amid the desolation of Kmart and the one-dollar shops. I found my heat beads and, feeling that my equilibrium had been slightly restored, headed home.

A week later and another weekend without Beck loomed. Before the unease of a lonely weekend had the opportunity to take hold, Beck's niece Belinda invited me to the races. Apart from the rodeo and the occasional barbecue at Belinda's, this was the first thing I had been invited to in the six months we'd been in Mount Isa.

I paid my twenty-dollar entry fee and went straight to the bar for a drink, where I was redirected to the ticket booth. In Queensland, it's not uncommon at public events to have to buy tickets for drinks and even for food. Then you take your ticket to another booth and exchange it for the consumable you require. This strange quirk of Queensland's liquor licensing laws not only forces double handling, but means you have to know in advance how many drinks you're going to consume, and what type. I did the maths – I'll probably stay two to three hours, and I'm driving, so three mid-strength beers will do me – and bought three XXXX Gold tickets.

Belinda was already there with Seppo, some of his relatives and a few mates. He did the introductions. 'This is my uncle Tony from Melbourne.'

One fella shook my hand. 'You're from Melbourne?'

I nod. Technically I'm from Adelaide, but this didn't seem the time for technicalities.

'That makes you a Prictorian then, eh,' he taunted with a laugh.

I grimaced and turned away, not wishing to engage in further conversation with him or others in his party, and slowly sipped my beer.

I'm not a regular frequenter of the races but some of my earliest and fondest childhood memories are of going to the Easter Oakbank races in the Adelaide Hills when my dad was still alive. As a family we would pile into the blue Valiant station wagon and head out of town to be joined by cousins and other families for a large rambling picnic under the trees next to the track. We'd spend hours playing in the creek and surrounding bush, circling back to the picnic occasionally for food and drink, paying little interest to the races.

Belinda joined me. 'Sorry about that,' she said.

'It's okay. I'm not in a very social mood,' I replied.

After a few moments Belinda told me she was going to place a bet. 'How about you?' she asked.

'Yeah, maybe in a tick.'

Belinda left me to my own devices and went to place her bet – and no doubt find some better company. I scanned the stark racetrack and tight groups of friends huddled around the bar. Feeling like I didn't belong, I finished my beer and left.

So much for my afternoon out. When I got home I realised I still had two beer tickets in my pocket. So much for my maths.

I don't have to wait long before I'm called into surgery. I guess I must be in a different queue to the others, who are still leafing through out-of-date magazines or playing with their phones. The orderlies put me on a gurney and wheel me down a corridor, where I'm left waiting for another half-hour. There's some drama about the power in one of the operating rooms, I'm told, and there is a possibility my operation will be called off. With rising annoyance, I start to expect that I'll have to go through this whole procedure another day, but then the anaesthetist turns up. He makes some idle chatter about Melbourne, asks me to count down from ten, and I drift off.

I feel disgusting when I wake a few hours later. 'Everything went to plan,' the nurse tells me. 'You'll need to stay here until you pass water, and then you can go. But someone will have to pick you up.'

'I live with my mother-in-law,' I say. 'She doesn't drive, and my wife's out of town. I'll get a taxi.'

'No can do – you'll have to call someone. What about a work colleague or a friend?'

I nod obediently.

In between drifting off to sleep, I try to drink as much water as I can so that I piss. I feel nauseous from the anaesthetic and am in considerable pain.

Around 6 pm I finally manage a small wee and get the all clear. I suddenly remember that the meeting will have started, and text Bernice:

I'm just being let out and I'm in too much pain. I won't make it.

Don't worry, she replies; she has organised for a colleague to be on the line from Brisbane to answer any legal questions. Evidently Bernice knew right from the start I wouldn't make the meeting.

I ring Belinda and ask her to pick me up. She's confused. 'What happened?'

'It's okay, just a day op. I'll explain when you get here.'

I tell the nurse my niece is coming and they release me. I gingerly make my way down to the ground floor and out the front doors. A wave of nausea hits me at the entrance and I vomit into a bin just as Belinda pulls up.

'Why didn't you tell me?' she asks. 'I would've come earlier.'

I can tell she's hurt that I didn't let on and I feel sheepish.

Belinda helps me into the house. Diana sees instantly that I'm not as shipshape as I thought I'd be, and gets out of her chair and shuffles into the kitchen. 'I've made soup.'

'I don't think I can manage soup, but some dry biscuits and water would be great.'

I collapse on the couch and let Diana tend to me. The next morning I'm too unwell to go to work and give over to Diana's care. She rises to the occasion in remarkable fashion, and spends the day making me cups of tea and bringing me lunch and snacks, while I languish on the couch.

Diana and I slip into an easy companionship, as we tend to whenever Beck goes away. It's not that Beck's presence creates tension, but something happens between us when Beck's out of town. I'm not blood. I'm not the one who chides her when she eats too many sweets or doesn't exercise. I don't pull her up when she's emotionally withdrawn. That's Beck's job, the tasks of the daughter. This allows a sense of ease to settle between us.

Diana and I weren't always close. It took us quite a few years to find a way to understand each other. I used to think it was because four months into my relationship with Beck, I broke it off. Beck was heartbroken, and no parent likes to see their child in despair. Diana, like Beck, had to learn to trust that I wouldn't do that again, which they both did.

The distance between us was, I suspect, more to do with culture. I grew up in a middle-class, urban Catholic household. Diana grew up in a poor, rural Anglican household. My mother's father was

Italian, and my mother was by nature warm and demonstrative. I'm a man who talks about emotions, works with blackfellas and votes Green. Diana, by nature, is reserved and has lived her life in the bush, most of it in a hard mining town, where men work, drink and go piggin', and don't talk about emotions. We come from different worlds.

Not long before Beck went to Melbourne she was sitting at the kitchen table and Diana was shuffling back to her chair, and for some reason she stopped behind Beck and placed her hands on Beck's shoulders. I saw this out of the corner of my eye and a small charge went through me. It dawned on me that I had no memory of ever seeing Diana touch Beck before, apart from farewell and greeting hugs and the like, and I was shocked by the touch – and by the realisation that I was shocked. 'Don't be ridiculous!' Beck said when I raised this with her later that night. 'She often touches me affectionately.' I let it drop.

Diana and I have never discussed the tragedy of Michael's life, the deaths he was responsible for – the hit-and-run victim on the Gold Coast, his own son and then himself. She barely acknowledges her grief with Beck, let alone with me. But I'm aware that these events led her to close down somewhat, to withdraw to such an extent that her sharp wit became dulled. But now, living with her, I see glimpses of it more and more, especially when Beck is around. Diana is peeling off the layers. They both are, in fact. Whether it's all the sun or being back in her childhood home and living with her mum – or perhaps it's menopause – Beck is letting her natural joyful countenance shine, and this is rubbing off on her mum.

I hobble into the kitchen just as Diana is about to pour some whisky into a pot on the stove. 'What are you doing?' I ask.

'Making corned beef,' she says.

'With whisky?'

'Of course not. Vinegar.' Diana peers closely at the bottle. 'Oh, I see.' She laughs. 'That would have made it interesting.'

'Disgusting, I reckon.'

'Yes, I suspect you're right.'

I get the vinegar from the cupboard, hand it to Diana and take the whisky from her. 'I better have a shot.'

'Medicinal purposes,' Diana retorts.

'Of course. How about yourself?'

'No, thank you.'

By the end of the second day I'm feeling much better and challenge Diana to a game of Upwords. I win, just. I say goodnight and head to bed. As I walk down the hall I hear her humming a tuneless warble. I smile. I text Beck from bed:

I don't think your mum's going anywhere in a hurry.

Beck replies:
I better come back then.

I text:
Only if you want xxx

7

A FRESH START

Rebecca

The excitement of nearly being home begins with my first glimpse of the Selwyn Range. From my seat on the plane I can see its seams stretching across the land. They are made up of red hills with almost rounded tops. Sprinkled across the hills are sparse gums and gidgee. I can tell there has been a bit of rain as there's a green tinge across the landscape, and between the hills I can see pools of water. It looks quite fresh but even when it's dry and bleak, which is most of the year, I find it beautiful. The landscape is so familiar, and for me it's home.

I shut my eyes and lean my head against the window. I have been awake for over twenty-four hours and feel pretty average.

I have travelled a lot over the past few months, and am keen to get back to Tony, Mum and Madang Street and settle back into a routine. Before Christmas I worked on two shows in Melbourne, and then I spent Christmas on the Gold Coast with Georgina, her boyfriend and Tony's family. Now it's early February and I'm returning from two weeks' travel around Japan with Lucille.

In the last twenty-four hours I have flown from Tokyo to Cairns to Townsville, and I'm now on the last leg to Mount Isa.

Tomorrow I start a drama project for Disability Services, and later in the week I begin my contract social work position at Mount Isa Headspace as the partnership broker. It's a research and development project looking at mental health in the workplace. I feel as though, at last, I am over the unemployment hump.

I open my tray table and take out my diary. For the last few weeks I have been compiling a list of New Year's resolutions. I do this most Januarys but rarely keep to the resolutions for more than a few days. There have been times when I've thought I may as well just go down to the local gym, donate $500 and tell them I'll see them again the following January. It would save me a lot of angst. Regardless, compiling lists, be they of resolutions or tasks, is something I have always done.

My current list has all the regular 'mores' – more exercise, singing, dancing, reading, writing, gardening and loving. I think the most therapeutic part is simply putting pen to paper. It forces me to take a moment to think and reflect. I really do want to have more of these 'mores' in my life, yet I suspect that I'll just watch more episodes of my favourite shows instead.

I go back to looking out the window. The ground is zigzagged with tracks and trails that appear to lead nowhere. From up here the landscape seems to stretch on forever without any sign of life. This is harsh country. Over the years I've heard many stories of people who have been lost or gone missing in the bush. I have great respect for the wilderness but I am not afraid of it. As kids we were taken into the bush to waterholes and creeks, where we would swim and have picnics. We were introduced to it as a place to respect.

Mum has always loved the bush and has no fear of it either. I find this a bit surprising, as when she was a little girl she got lost in the bush for two nights and three days. It was April 1928, and Mum was four years old and at a church picnic in Coradgery West, sixteen miles from Trundle, in central New South Wales. She was with her father and two younger siblings, Hilary and Mary. Her mother was in hospital, having just given birth to a baby girl.

'The older children were playing hide and seek,' Mum once told me. 'I had never played it before and didn't know the rules. I watched the other children darting in and out of the bush around the picnic area and thought it was a chasing game.'

Mum took off into the scrub. She ran for a long time and finally found a burnt-out stump and hid behind it. She couldn't see any of the other children and felt pleased at how well she was doing in the game. After a short time she took off again and kept running further into the bush. She didn't notice how far she had gone until the light started to fade.

Back at the picnic ground, people began to pack up. Mum's father noticed she was missing. No one knew where she was. Things escalated quickly: search parties of men were assembled and the women organised food and drink for the searchers. My grandfather gathered together a prayer group in the hope that his fervent belief would provoke a miracle and his daughter would be found.

For two nights and three days Mum wandered through the bush. I asked her what she remembered.

'I drank water from the puddles,' she said.

'Were you scared?'

'I remember being scared once. I saw the search party on horses and they had lanterns.'

'Were they calling out your name?'

'I don't know,' she said. 'I ran off and hid.'

'Where did you sleep?'

'I tucked myself in under some bushes.'

In town, the men started making plans to dredge the surrounding dams, and trackers were called in to help find the little lost girl. At the hospital, Mum's mother was frantic with worry – and then the unthinkable happened. A nurse dropped the newborn baby girl, Pauline, and she died.

'Oh god!' I said. 'That's so awful! What was that like when you found out?'

'I don't remember.'

I found this really strange. Mum has an excellent memory, particularly for things from years ago. I didn't want to pathologise the experience, but it seemed impossible not to think about the effects of trauma on memory.

'You don't remember your parents telling you?' I asked.

'We didn't talk about things like that.'

'What – things like death?'

Mum didn't answer.

'But didn't you wonder where the baby was?'

Again she didn't answer.

'You must have known that your mother was pregnant and going to have a baby?'

'I have no recollection of being aware of it one way or the other,' she said at last.

'But it must have affected your mother?'

'Mum was never particularly maternal.'

'What do you mean?'

Mum shrugged and was silent for a moment. 'My parents were probably ill-suited to each other,' she said. 'Dad was a religious intellectual and Mum liked dances, horse riding, gardening and playing cards.'

Later, I asked Mum's sister Mary about this time, and she told me that she thought the loss of the baby affected their mother's mental health. 'Mum was never very affectionate or warm with us,' she said. 'She was prone to outbursts of temper and ignoring us, yet would lavish attention on other people's children.'

Their very pious and staunch Anglican minister father was, from all accounts, not particularly emotive either. He was committed to the church and ensuring that his children were well educated. Although born and raised in St Kilda, in Melbourne, my grandfather seemed to find some kind of solace in rural and remote Queensland. He moved the family to Aramac, in central Queensland, and became a travelling minister for a diocese that spread over a large area. He was often away for long stretches of time.

Aunty Mary talked about this as a fairly unpleasant time, and she missed her father a great deal. 'I seemed to irritate Mum, and she didn't want me around,' she told me. 'Dad ended up taking me with him on his circuit, and I was much happier when I was with him.'

I have often wondered if my grandmother would have been happier married to someone who worked the land rather than a minister.

'She liked the status of being married to a minister,' Aunty Mary told me, 'but it was hard work. She spent a lot of her time raising money for the church and doing things for other people but we often missed out.'

Eventually my grandparents separated. I suspect this caused them great shame; it was certainly not the done thing. I have often wondered if this was the reason Mum stuck by Dad for all those years. There were certainly times when I questioned why on earth they had chosen to stay together as they both seemed so miserable.

Silence is a recurring theme in my family. I think back to the death of my little nephew, Michael Pancho, just before his first birthday, and remember the silence that surrounded that tragedy. As with the disappearance of my brother, nobody spoke about it. I can remember feeling gutted and confused. It was so unfair.

How could such a sweet and happy little baby die like that, so unintentionally?

I was in Year 11 at the time. My best friend, Lisa, had been diagnosed with leukaemia and was very sick. These two things threw me into a sort of existential crisis. I began to feel ambivalent about school, and wondered what the point of anything was.

I decided to leave school at the end of the year, and applied for an apprenticeship as an electrician at the mines. I had spent a lot of time sitting in my room taking apart my radio, calculator and cassette player, so I thought perhaps I would enjoy that sort of thing. In reality I was taking things apart because I was bored and frustrated, not because I was particularly interested in electronics.

I received news that I had been accepted into the trade at the end of the school year, and I think that this was all I needed to turn things around. I didn't want to be an electrician; I just wanted to know that there was something else out there beyond my family and our grief.

I went back to school and began Year 12, and then Lisa died. But for once there was not silence. Mum knew I was fragile, and she spent hours with me gently talking about life and loss. Dad even rallied and acknowledged that he understood my grief. I suspect that Lisa was far enough removed from both of them that they were able to offer empathy. Regardless, it was what I needed. Though deeply saddened by the death of my adorable friend, I found my feet again and got on with school and all that was happening around me.

And the little lost girl?

'After three days I wandered into a homestead on a property ten miles from where I went missing,' Mum told me. 'My feet were cut and bleeding, and the elastic in my bloomers was broken but I had clung to the top of them for the three days so that they wouldn't fall off. For months after being found I had to have physiotherapy each day, with a wooden peg, to release the closed grip that my fingers and fist had formed.' Holding a pen in her hand, Mum showed me how she had to work it along her palm and down her fingers.

At the homestead, the grazier picked Mum up and said to his wife, 'I have found the little lost girl.'

In what became a favourite family quote, Mum replied, 'No, I have found myself.'

As we fly over the ranges, I add to my list in my diary: 'Take Mum out bush more.'

Mum loves going for drives out bush, sitting under a tree, having a cup of tea and doing a crossword or just watching the landscape. I am aware that over the past few months I've found all sorts of excuses to not do this: too busy, too hot, too hard.

A couple of years ago, Mum had a fall in the car park of the Buffs Club as she was getting into Belinda's four-wheel drive, and since then she has refused to travel in anything other than a sedan. She was hurt and embarrassed by the fall, and it rocked her confidence. I know I've used this as a reason not to head out for afternoon drives. It's a pretty lame excuse, though, as there are lots of places we can go to that don't need a four-wheel drive.

As kids, we used to go out to creeks and waterholes and we never had a four-wheel drive then. We also spent a lot of time roaming around the bushland on the outskirts of town, and entire afternoons playing in the scrub down the creek. I don't recall Mum ever checking up on us or telling us to take water, a hat or shoes, or warning us about 'stranger danger'. We were never alone, and it was just assumed that we had enough common sense to look after ourselves.

December 1966. I was four years old, and was playing on the swing in the backyard with my brother David. Mum was burning rubbish in the incinerator. It was hot and sunny, and I was wearing a yellow A-line shift that Mum had made.

My grandmother was in town, staying at my cousins' house. I had only just met her for the first time, so she was a big attraction. I hadn't heard much about her other than that she lived for a number of years in Alice Springs, and more recently in London. I knew London from the poem 'Pussy Cat, Pussy Cat', and so in my mind Grandma was as good as related to the Queen, hence my desire to spend time with her.

I swung back and forwards on the swing set and whined, 'When are we going to visit Grandma?'

Mum had answered this question quite a few times, so didn't give me much of a response.

'When?' I asked again.

'Maybe when Dad gets home after work,' she said at last. 'Or maybe on the weekend.'

'I want to go now!'

Mum and David ignored me.

I remember standing at the back gate. I wasn't wearing shoes. We never wore shoes around the house or when we played; no one did. I said to Mum and David, 'I'm going to visit Grandma!'

Mum took no notice of me. She continued to burn things in the incinerator, and David kept playing on the swing.

So I headed off down the street to visit Grandma. No one tried to stop me.

I didn't get very far. At the end of the street a woman called out to me, 'Where are you going, little girl?'

'To visit my grandmother.'

'Where does she live?'

'Down there.' I pointed towards the Barkly Highway.

The woman came out of her yard. 'What's your name?'

'Rebecca.'

'Would you like to come in for a glass of cordial and a biscuit, Rebecca?'

I liked the sound of that and went into the woman's house. She gave me some cordial and a biscuit. While I ate and drank, she made a phone call. I didn't know who she was talking to, but she said my name and 'Soldiers Hill'. I knew that I lived in Soldiers Hill.

After the phone call, the woman asked, 'Would you like to help me with the housework?'

I liked helping Mum with the housework, so I said yes. I didn't tell the woman that I really only liked three housework jobs, and they were polishing ornaments, dusting, and putting the washing through the ringer on top of the washing machine, but I was only allowed to do that with Mum's assistance.

Whenever I helped Mum, I only had to do it for a short time, and then we'd have a tea break. That was the part of helping that I liked the most.

'Great – you can help me make the beds!' the woman said. She smiled a lot. I didn't like making beds but I didn't tell the woman this. She seemed quite excited so I wondered if it might be more fun than bed-making at my own home.

The woman asked a lot of questions. She wanted to know how old I was, if I had brothers and sisters, where my dad worked, if I went to school. I could answer most of the questions but I didn't know where Dad worked. 'He makes the smoke come out of the stack,' I told her.

The woman laughed. 'Really?'

I nodded, because this was what Dad had told me, pointing to the smelter stack as he did.

I forgot all about visiting Grandma. Eventually we finished

making the beds and went into the lounge. I wondered if it might be tea break time.

There was a knock at the door, and I saw Mum standing on the verandah. At first I was disappointed as things were going so well with the woman that I thought I might stay for longer. But I was also excited to see Mum, because I thought perhaps Mum and the woman would become friends. In my mind this was quite logical. The woman liked housework and Mum liked housework so it seemed a good match. Mum came into the house.

'You must have been worried sick?' the woman said to her.

I didn't follow what Mum said, as all I could think was that something bad had happened at home. Why else would Mum be worried?

'She's a good little helper,' the woman says.

I smiled shyly. I liked the flattery but already knew that it was not the done thing to bask in praise.

Mum agreed. They talked some more and then we said goodbye.

The woman said, 'You can drop in any time, Rebecca, and help me with the housework.'

I smiled but didn't say anything. I knew I wouldn't be back. I wasn't interested in her housework jobs: too boring and no tea break.

As Mum and I walked home, I said, 'I wasn't really going to walk to Grandma's.'

'I know,' Mum said.

'I was just going to walk around the block.'

Again Mum said, 'I know.' It never crossed my mind to ask how she knew where I was.

When I got home I was allowed to have another glass of cordial and a biscuit. I was pretty happy about that. My visit to the woman's house was never mentioned again.

Years later, Mum told me that the woman had called in to

a radio station, saying there was a little lost girl called Rebecca, with blonde hair, found roaming the streets in Soldiers Hill. Mum's neighbour heard this and came over and told Mum.

'But I wasn't lost,' I said to Mum.

'I know,' she said.

I did eventually get to spend time with my grandma, and though I knew I was not her favourite grandchild we were good mates. I loved visiting her when she moved to Cloncurry and became manager of the CWA hostel. There was something curious and mysterious about her that I could never quite put my finger on. She was very much her own person, but also had an old-fashioned formality about her. She had olive skin, an aquiline nose and long hair that she wore in a chignon at the back of her head. I was fair, burnt easily and had wispy blonde hair that was never going to be pulled into anything other than a scrawny pigtail.

I went to my first high school dance when I was twelve and in Year 8. All week we had watched preparations being made. The dance was going to happen on the school tennis courts, and large sheets of hessian were hung across the tall wire fences to create a private space. The tennis nets and umpires' seats were removed, and party lights were strung around the courts. A huge PA system was trucked in.

On Friday night the courts were packed. It felt like every kid at school had turned up. The dance went off – there was smoking and kissing and fighting and sneaky drinking. I had never seen anything like it. My friends and I spent most of our time hiding up the back, just watching the antics. The PA pumped out all the latest hits, and although it was overwhelming it was also exhilarating.

Grandma was at our house when David and I got home from the dance. 'How was the orchestra?' she asked.

This question reduced David and me to hysterics. We laughed so much we couldn't speak.

'You are both rude and very silly,' said Grandma, sucking on one of her many Alpine cigarettes. As a teenager, I stole these cigarettes from her and smoked them down the creek with my friends. I hated the taste, but thoroughly enjoyed the naughtiness of it.

Like Mum, Grandma loved the bush. My favourite trips into the bush as a kid were in Cloncurry with Grandma. We'd pick her up from the CWA hostel and head down the riverbed for a picnic. Grandma would always stick her head out the window of the car and say, 'Can you smell the gidgee?'

I would stick my head out and inhale deeply, but I was never sure what I was trying to smell. Grandma and Mum could also smell when a storm was coming. As I grew up, I eventually got the sense of these smells as well.

Down at the creek, Dad would make a fire, boil the billy and make tea. Mum would slice the fruitcake and get out a tin of homemade biscuits. Sometimes we would stay until after sunset. I loved this time. Mum and Grandma would talk about books and recite poetry. The evening shadows and the light of the fire gave me confidence, and I too would recite.

My favourite poem when I was twelve was an extract from 'Ballad of the Mari Lwyd' by Vernon Watkins. This poem is very long but my speech and drama teacher had given me a section of it to learn as an example of rhythm and onomatopoeia.

The poem is based on an old Welsh custom that was supposed to bring good luck. A party of people, usually men, would accompany a person disguised as a horse and go from house to house. At each house they would knock on the door, call out and sing in the hope of being let in. If they were let in, they would be rewarded with food and drink, and would sing a bit more before going on to another house.

What I loved was the sound of the words and the rhythm. The word *midnight* is used as a recurring refrain. My teacher encouraged me to enunciate clearly, but also quickly to create the sense of a galloping horse. I loved it.

In the light of the fire I recited this poem for my family. I thought it was a pretty normal thing to do until my cousin mocked me in the shadows by repeatedly saying, 'Midnight, midnight, midnight, midnight ...' I guess I was fair game. I was innocent and very much in love with the magic of words, and I wore that love on my sleeve. When you're twelve, that's asking for trouble. I was also right on the cusp of adolescence, and developing a teenage self-consciousness and acute sensitivity. My cousin's teasing literally stopped me in my tracks. I wouldn't recite poetry aloud again until I was an adult.

As we begin our descent to Mount Isa, I can see the famous smelter stacks looming on the horizon. These are the signposts of the town, and everyone who lives here has a story about how and when they first saw the stacks. For many years there was a popular T-shirt with a picture of the stacks in a car's rear-view mirror with the words 'The Best View of Mount Isa'.

The flight into 'the Isa' is quite spectacular. Depending on which way you fly in, you either get an incredible view of the landscape or of the mine. Regardless of your feelings about the scar that the mine creates across the side of the town, it's impossible not to be struck by its size and complexity. This huge industrial monolith stretches for a couple of kilometres across the western side of town, and the tunnels in the area go for miles. The mine is like a city within itself, and although I'm not a fan of the mining industry, the magnitude of the place is impressive.

As a kid, I assumed that all towns had a mine. I remember being surprised on a childhood holiday at the Gold Coast. I kept looking around for some form of industry, and more specifically a mine. I couldn't fathom that a place could operate without a mine. What did people do for jobs?

When you leave the outskirts of Mount Isa, you don't see another town for a good hour or so until you hit Mary Kathleen; drive a bit further through the bush and you hit Cloncurry; then you go through the scrub again and find yourself in Julia Creek. The boundaries are clear – but on the Gold Coast it felt like one elongated place. Broadbeach ran into Mermaid Beach, which ran into Miami Beach, and so on. How did people know where they came from? How did they know who was part of their mob? I found these things very perplexing, and was always relieved to get back to Mount Isa, the mine and the clear boundaries that marked out our town.

I left home when I was seventeen and moved away from the bush. First I was an exchange student for a year in the United States, and when I returned I moved to Brisbane to go to university. Over the years, I lived in Brisbane, Boonah, Woodridge, Darwin, Daylesford, Melbourne – and now I've come back to Mount Isa.

Before I came back, I think my love of the bush had become more romantic nostalgia than fact. At times it saddens me to think how urban I've become. But then out of the blue something would happen that would remind me of my roots.

I remember a family lunch in February 2010. I was listening to a conversation between my brother-in-law Paul and his friend Brian. They were discussing a friend of theirs.

'I heard he's in Paris,' Brian said.

'What's he doing?' asked Paul.

'Apparently he's doing a lot of fencing,' says Brian.

I was very surprised to hear this. I've been to Paris a couple of times, I think to myself, and I've never seen anyone doing any fencing. In fact, I can't recall ever seeing any fences in Paris ... 'He's doing fencing?' I asked incredulously.

Yes, they told me.

'Really?' I asked. 'In *Paris*?'

'Fencing originated in France,' Paul said.

I was even more surprised to hear this – I had no idea. This conversation was strange but also quite illuminating.

Paul continued: 'Lots of the terms used in fencing are French.'

'What, like *ratchet*?' I asked, miming someone tightening a fence wire.

'No,' Paul said, 'like *engarde* and *épée*.' He mimes holding out a fencing foil.

The penny dropped. They meant the fine art of fencing! I burst out laughing. As hip and urban as I think I am, I will always think that *fencing* means a bale of wire, utes and post-hole diggers!

The air steward announces that it's time to put up my tray table, put my seat into the upright position and prepare for landing. I do all these things but hold on to my diary. I want to add something more before I land. I feel there must be something I need to attend to before the year takes off, and I want to make sure I note it down.

With a year of experience of caring for Mum under my belt, I feel ready for what the next twelve months will bring. But I'm also keen to do something more with and for Mum. I know I will maintain all the day-to-day things, but I keep wondering if there's something else I should be doing.

For a while now I've been thinking that maybe I should make some recordings of Mum telling stories. There are still so many things I don't know about my family, and I wonder whether the best way to do this would be by recording an oral history. I've worked on projects like that before, and in fact have recently received funding to do a series of interviews for a new play that I'm writing about suicide.

Mum is often reluctant to talk about things from the past, but maybe if I present it to her as a way of documenting our family history she might be more inclined. I'm not sure, but I make a note of it in my diary.

April 1979. I was sixteen and hanging out with my cousin Bronwyn at her house. It was a school night and I was still wearing my uniform. I loved spending time at this house. It was cool and calm, and I loved my aunty Veronica, uncle Vince and my cousins. We'd all grown up together, and they'd have seen the best and the worst of my family.

Veronica was one of those people who laughs a lot. Vince, who escaped Czechoslovakia during World War II, was creative, and was the first person I knew who did stencilling. He had made beautiful artworks on the walls of their house, and on fabric that he made into curtains and cushion covers. This intrigued me. My dad didn't make art or use the sewing machine!

Mum and Veronica were sisters, and were very close. When we were little we all spent lots of time together on the weekends, at the swimming pool or the dam or out bush having picnics.

We were all much older now, but Bronwyn and I still sought each other out for friendship. She had spent the last few years at boarding school, but was now back home in Mount Isa. I liked having her around. We didn't live in each other's pocket, but we had an ease that came from familiarity.

It was a hot night and we were all crowded around the lounge room air conditioner. My aunty Mary from Rockhampton and my uncle Hilary from Brisbane were also visiting. My brother Paul was home from university.

Grandma, who had left Cloncurry by now and was living in one of the semi-independent units of the aged care facility in Mount Isa, had had a stroke and was in hospital. She couldn't go back to her unit as she needed daily nursing, and this wasn't provided by the facility. Mum and her siblings were discussing what needed to happen for Grandma, where she would live and who would look after her.

Suddenly voices were raised and Aunty Veronica spoke loudly and sharply to her siblings. I caught a fraction of what was being said and wanted to hear more, but Paul grabbed my arm and shuffled Bronwyn and me out of the room. He told us to go into the back room and watch TV. I could hear the raised voices but couldn't make anything out.

A short time later my brother returned and told me we were going. We left quickly; no one said goodbye. Mum, Paul, Aunty Mary and I got into the Kingswood and Paul drove us home. No one spoke. It was strange, but I knew enough of the ways of my family to say nothing.

When we got home, Mum and Aunty Mary went into my parents' room and shut the door. No one in my family ever shut doors. All discussion, arguments and fights were held in the lounge room or the kitchen. I'd slammed doors on my parents but they never hid what was being discussed. No doubt they'd had many discussions after I was asleep, but at sixteen I was only aware of what happened in my waking world. And in that world all doors were open.

The days drifted on, and as per usual no one spoke about what had happened at my cousins' house. Grandma came out of hospital and came to live with us. She was partially paralysed and needed twenty-four-hour care. She had lost a lot of her language skills, and Mum spent hours playing Scrabble with her as a way to encourage her to think and speak. The Blue Nurses came every few days and helped with showering and toileting, but mainly it was Mum, Dad and his sister Eileen who did the work.

Thirty-seven years have now passed. Grandma has been dead for thirty-five of those, but my aunty Veronica and uncle Vince have not seen or spoken to my family since that night in their house. Over the years I've tried to get Mum to tell me what happened but she won't. I tried with Aunty Mary too, but she just said, 'Sometimes things are better left as water under the bridge.' I thought that was mixing metaphors, but I didn't say it. I pleaded but Mum and her sister were adamant. The past was past.

Over the years, Bronwyn and I have circled in and out of each other's lives. We both know that we like each other, and we both want something from each other, but we also know that the past can be painful. I have beautiful memories of her playing the piano. She would play 'Little Boxes' for me, and I would skip around the lounge singing the words. It's been years since I've heard her play.

We've both tried hard to make our relationship work, but there's always an elephant in the corner – the hurt of our parents, the unspoken silence between our mothers. Bronwyn and I don't talk about it either. I want to, but perhaps I am more like my mother than I'm prepared to admit. Perhaps I too am uncomfortable with confronting past hurts, so am also prepared to let it go.

The plane starts to circle the town, and I can see our house in Soldiers Hill. Slowly we descend to the airport on the outskirts of town. It's just after 7 pm and I know Tony will be waiting for me.

I leave the plane and walk across the tarmac towards the arrivals area. Although it's early evening, it is still murderously hot but I don't care. I can see Tony grinning broadly through the glass doors. I wave and rush towards him.

Tony wraps me in a huge hug. The last few months have been hard on him, I know. He hasn't complained but he's had to do lot of the caring of Mum by himself as I've had so many trips away. He takes it all in his stride but I know he has missed me, and at times has been lonely and bored. While I was in Japan he sent me an email telling me about a story he was thinking of writing about a man who is abandoned by his wife and has to remain caring for his mother-in-law. We both agree it would make a great story, but that it would be just that – a story. I ain't going anywhere!

Mum shuffles to the back door as the car pulls into the driveway. As I open the car door she steps out onto the back landing. 'Hello, daughter!' she calls.

'Hello, mother!' I laugh.

I look up and see that Mum has a huge smile across her face. She is wearing her special muu-muu and her hair looks freshly combed. This is a good sign. I get my suitcase and head up the back ramp. Mum waits at the top and gives me a huge hug. I go inside and take my suitcase to the bedroom. Everything looks so neat and clean, and the air conditioner hums gently. It feels so different from when we arrived twelve months ago.

We sit down to dinner, and Mum runs through a list of questions: 'How was Luci? Was it cold? Did it rain? Did you only eat Japanese food? Did you see cherry blossoms? How were the trains?' Mum has always loved travel, and is a great person to chat with after a trip. Lots of people barely acknowledge that you've been away but Mum always wants all the details.

I pull out the gifts I've brought home. Most of them are food. Mum tries the matcha chocolate and the matcha mochi, and after a few samples announces that she does not like either. She does, however, like the various flavours of KitKat and other chocolate goodies. I give her some beautiful writing paper and tell her about the stationery shop we visited in Tokyo. Tony gets duty-free whisky, chocolate and socks.

After dinner, though I am exhausted, I play a welcome home game of Upwords with Mum. She slaughters me and is very pleased with herself. I am almost delirious with tiredness so I don't mind at all.

At last I get into bed. Tony reaches down under the bed and pulls out a large wrapped parcel and hands it to me.

'What's this?' I ask.

'Something you've talked about for ages,' he says.

I can't for the life of me think what it is. I sit in bed and pull the paper off. Tony watches me, looking excited.

As I rip the paper, I can see the curve of a zip. I take off more paper and see an instrument bag. Inside is a ukulele.

'You've been talking about learning to play something for years,' Tony says. 'Now's the time.'

I take the ukulele out and look at it.

'Do you like it?' he asks.

I nod and smile and give it a few strums. 'Thank you.'

'I thought you could find songs that Diana likes and play them for her,' he says.

I smile. 'Yeah, I like the sound of that.'

It's true that I've been talking for years about playing something again. As a teenager I mucked around on the guitar, but I lost interest when the going got tough. Dad had always wanted me to learn to play the piano but for some reason I turned my back on it. It is now one of my biggest regrets.

I think Tony's right: now does feel like the right time to give something new a try. I find my diary, open it and add to my list: 'Learn to play the ukulele.'

I thank Tony and we turn off the light. I lie in the dark and listen to the hum of the air conditioner.

And so year two begins. I feel very content. Like Mum, all those years ago, I think I may have found myself.

8

SALUTING THE SUN

Tony

I'm up early. Beck comes home today on the evening flight and I'm excited.

Yesterday I'd woken up to discover Diana had had an accident, and there was poo on the floor of the toilet and the bathroom. I cleaned it up with toilet paper and mopped the floor with hot water and Dettol while Diana had her morning cup of tea in her chair. I discreetly checked her room and the laundry basket: all was fine. It was the first time this had happened when Beck was not around. I was unsure what to do. Until now this had been Beck's domain. Diana said nothing about it, and she didn't smell so I decided not to say anything either – but I remained vigilant.

'I don't think she was aware,' I reported to Beck in an email.

'It's good I'm home tomorrow,' Beck replied.

She's right. I'm ready for her return, and I think Diana is too. We miss the energy and colour that Beck brings, and I worry about the long days for Diana when I'm at work, especially on those days when I don't come home for lunch and Diana has no outings planned. Yet I firmly believe that Beck's trip to Japan with Lucille was vital for the sustainability of this arrangement. Not only would it help keep Beck sane, but it'd also reassure the kids that we're still able to spend time with them. That we haven't abandoned them. They might be young adults, but they still want and need their parents. But I want and need Beck back here too.

'We'll leave in ten,' I tell Diana, who is ready for church; in fact, she has been ready for some time, and is patiently reading a large-print book in her chair.

Marj swings opens the gate as we arrive at the church. 'No climbing over for me these days,' she says. Marj has had hip surgery and walks with difficulty.

'But what if I want to?' Diana quips.

'You could pray for a miracle and do it when I pick you up,' I say. I take my hand away and Marj holds out her arm to Diana.

I want to go to yoga, but I have to come back here to pick up Diana in an hour so I can't. It's been a couple of months since I've been, and I'm missing it. I remember clearly the last time I went. It was close to 6 pm but still over forty degrees. It had been that way for weeks, and summer had barely begun. Janine sounded the gong, signalling that it was time to get up from the mat and move into the lotus position. Now for three Oms – the affirmation of the divine presence.

I like the sound of the Om – the resonance of the different voices coming together – but despite nearly twenty years of practice, I'm still not completely comfortable with the chanting part of yoga. I'm too self-consciousness and, having eschewed religion years ago, I'm not inclined to affirm any divine presence.

That evening I'd positioned myself against the wall. The air conditioner, even on high, didn't have the grunt to push much air my way, but at least I avoided the direct blast of the setting sun as it streamed in through the high windows and crossed the floor of the studio.

That night, in concession to the heatwave, the class focused on breath, keeping movement to a minimum. Janine instructed us to breathe into the abdomen deeply, diaphragm out. 'Breathe out completely, diaphragm in. Still the mind. Rest, relax, release.'

I need to be careful about relaxing too much; it's not uncommon for me to drift off during relaxation exercises. As is the case whenever I stop and pause for a while: at the movies, at meetings, at lectures (in my uni days), in front of the TV, at the theatre (much to Beck's chagrin – not that we've been to much theatre lately). So falling asleep at yoga's not surprising. Sometimes I defy Janine's instructions to still the mind, and instead allow my thoughts to run free so that I don't drift off. Too often I have come to, prone on the mat, to find the others poised and ready for the next pose.

My thoughts turned to Daylesford, where we lived for a decade. One year I signed up for a midwinter early-morning intensive program: two weeks of daily yoga. Leaving the snug bed, I'd swaddle myself in layers, including beanie and gloves, and head out into the cold, dark pre-dawn. Some mornings I'd have to pour water on the windscreen to remove the ice; other days the fog would be so thick I'd have to perch on the edge of the seat and peer through the window as the narrow beams of light guided me slowly down the hill. At the old weatherboard guesthouse I'd abandon the relative warmth of the car for the yoga room, which I knew would be cold, the little blow heater being no match for the cold seeping in through the cracks in the floorboards and the ill-fitting windows.

As Janine's soft lilt drew me back to the muggy present, I yearned for some of that cold. The long Mount Isa summer stretched before me like a heat mirage on a country road.

Finished with the breathing exercises, we were now saluting the sun. Sweat dripped from my forehead as I bent towards the mat. The sun, as if in acknowledgement, emerged from behind a cloud and poured in through the windows. Those who had opted to be under the air-conditioner vent in the centre of the room were now paying the price.

I gently stretched my hamstring as I brought my left leg forwards into a lunge. I was still feeling the effects of the tennis grand final two days before. Although Monday-night drop-in tennis had not continued, enough players were found for a Wednesday-night social competition. The game hadn't commenced until the last of the sun had disappeared behind the mine, but the heat had lingered like a (not so divine) presence, pulsating off the concrete courts. After two tie-breaks the match was evenly poised at one set all. Early in the third, my partner, who had given it his all, succumbed to heat exhaustion. I played on solo, eventually losing 6–3. I tried to dismiss the what-ifs – the just-out serves and the missed volleys – as I stretched my arms above my head and arched my back.

'Empty the mind,' Janine had exhorted. 'Rest, relax, release.'

The sun had moved on now, and those at the back of the room were bathed in a golden glow. Earlier that day Beck had come home to find Diana disoriented and bleeding from the head. As Beck unravelled the chain of events, it became apparent that Diana, after returning from her weekly visit to the nursing home, had passed out and hit her head again as she collapsed to the floor. The ambulance came and took her to the hospital; apparently she was dehydrated again. Of course, it wasn't uncommon for the elderly to die in this sort of heat; the obsession with hydration belongs to the young.

We moved on to our final chants. Again three Oms. After an hour and a half of yoga our voices were imbued with a languid richness. The Oms were followed by a prayer in Sanskrit recited by Janine. At the end of each line, most of the other students chanted a response. Clammy from sweat, I remained silent, but I could make out the faint sound of thunder in the distance. Bending forwards in thanks, with my hands against my heart, palms together, I offered a prayer for rain.

Sadly there is no time for yoga today, and I drive to Coles instead. I need to shop for Beck's homecoming dinner. She has requested 'a selection of salads'. Diana and I are not exactly thrilled at her choice, but we don't push back. After the shops I swing by the church. I'm earlier than usual and the service has only just finished. Not wanting Diana to feel hurried, I stay for a cup of tea and some cake. 'How are you enjoying Mount Isa?' the priest, Merlin, asks.

'The official or unofficial version?' I reply, glancing across at Diana with a smile.

'Whatever you like,' Merlin replies earnestly. I don't think he got the joke.

'Actually it's been good. We're looking forward to Beck getting home today. Aren't we, Diana?'

'Oh, I suppose,' says Diana, taking a cupcake from the plate proffered by a child.

'You don't mind the heat?' Merlin's assistant asks.

'Not really,' I say, trying hard not to stare at his impressive walrus moustache. 'It doesn't worry me, but I love it when we get the thunderstorms and rain.'

'Good for the garden,' Merlin replies. He and his wife also run the plant nursery in town – our go-to destination most weekends.

This season's rain came just before we went to the Gold Coast for a holiday with Georgina and her boyfriend. Beck's brother David and his three kids tag-teamed us and came up to Mount Isa to look after Diana over Christmas while we had some time away. After almost a year, we needed to take stock, and there's nothing like a week at the beach to make one feel completely at peace with the world. Poking around the rockpools at the base of the headland at sunset, we had no trouble recommitting to the Mount Isa project. We missed our girls in Melbourne but knew they were okay. We weren't unhappy, so why not stay? As twilight descended, we returned to our apartment buoyed by our newfound resolve – and by the prospect of a gin and tonic on the balcony overlooking the twinkling Gold Coast.

It was still raining when we got back to Mount Isa a week later. David and the kids had to delay their return as all the roads out were cut off. We didn't mind as it meant we got to spend a few days together, although with four extra bodies in it, the house was bursting at the seams.

I first got to know David in late 1990, when he, Beck and I went camping at the Gregory River and Lawn Hill Gorge. I was a university-educated city boy in my late twenties, wearing my black Akubra with a woven Murri band around the crown. David was very different from me – he left school early, worked in the mines and had lived in the north all his life – but he was very funny and a good conversationalist.

We hit it off instantly, though for some reason I had decided to call him 'Sunshine'. I'm not sure why. I must have heard the expression somewhere and thought it a good, blokey way to refer to someone. After a couple of days, he pulled me up and said, 'If you called someone in prison "Sunshine", it'd be a sure-fire way to get your head kicked in.' I took the hint.

After lunch on Boxing Day, we loaded up David's Toyota with camping gear and an esky full of beer and meat, and with the three us perched on the bench seat in the front we took off for the Gregory, about four hours north. We drank beer, smoked joints and sang as we drove. It was insanely hot, and the yellow-tinted sunglasses I was wearing infused the terrain with a soft, golden glow.

I was mindful of the fact that although I was a reasonably seasoned drinker, I was likely no match for David; I needed to pace myself. David had brought a bottle of Rebel Yell bourbon, which was tucked away in the back, and I suspected that once we set up camp it would appear. I was anxious that with bourbon on top of beers and joints, I would be a goner. I had my male pride and ego to manage: I didn't want David to think I was the soft city boy I really was.

Eventually, we pulled up at the Gregory Downs pub to get some ice for the esky. We had what I felt was half a cow in there, and the ice was running low. 'Out of ice,' the publican announced. We looked at each other in dismay.

We continued on to our camp site along the rough dirt road. Once there, I took off my sunglasses and instantly realised that evening was still a couple of hours away, and the creeping headache I felt told me I hadn't paced myself as well as I'd planned.

Bouncing along the rough track had jumbled all our gear in the back, and as David opened the back door the Rebel Yell came tumbling out. I was standing off to the side, and I watched the bottle fall. It spun end over end in what seemed like slow motion, and then clipped the tow bar. The bottle cracked open, and as it hit the sandy ground the amber liquid drained instantly away. David put his hands to his head and cried, 'Fuck, fuck, fuck!' Under my breath I muttered, 'You beauty!' I looked across at Beck and could see relief flood across her face too.

'We'd better eat all this meat,' David announced. 'It'll be fucked by the morning.' Beck had been vegetarian when I met her, and although she ate meat now our diet was still predominantly vego. But with no other option, we cooked up all the meat in the stinking heat and munched our way through it, chased down with joints and rapidly warming beers.

Later, David pulled a sawn-off .22 from under the seat of

the car. We were horrified. 'Ya never know who might be out in these parts,' he warned. 'If someone in what looks like a broken-down car waves you over, don't ever drive right up to 'em. Stop fifty yards away, and one of youse get out and walk up real slow, while the other stays in the car, gets the rifle out and has it at the ready.'

Appalled and thrilled in equal measure, we spent the rest of the night shooting cane toads as they encroached on our camp site. Eventually we went to bed. The heat didn't relent throughout the night, and at around 2 am all three of us crept, groaning from the semi-digested meat, out of our swags and into the river, where we lay in its shallow, tepid waters, vainly seeking relief.

There was no ice in the esky by the next morning and we had another carton of beer in the back of the car that we needed to chill. David had concluded that 'the prick' at the pub had had plenty of ice, but because we hadn't bought our beer from him he'd pretended otherwise. So we hatched a plan to go back and test David's theory. At midday, after spending the morning bemoaning the heat – and still feeling toxic from the beer, joints and astounding amount of meat we'd consumed the day before – we took ourselves off to the pub. From under the midday sun in the car park we could see into the dark reaches of the verandah, and beyond into the bar, which we imagined was significantly cooler than outside. We made a solemn pact before we got out of the car that it would be one lemon squash only. Enough for us to suss out the ice situation and get the hell out of there without giving the 'money-hungry grub' any more of our dough than we had to.

We settled into our stools at the bar and ordered our squashes. Icy cold, they slid down our throats quickly. We asked the publican what the temperature was. 'Forty-seven in here,' he said. 'Add a couple of degrees out there.' I was dumbfounded. Without hesitating, we ordered another round.

Once they were drained, we looked at each other and David said, 'One beer won't hurt.'

'Only one!' Beck and I chorused.

As we were drinking our beers, Shane Howard (of Goanna fame), his partner and children came into the bar. We struck up a conversation, and to be sociable we ordered another round of drinks. Then another, and another. The hot afternoon passed. Eventually, we determined that it must be time to head back to camp. 'We'll need some ice, thanks, mate,' David announced to the publican.

'Sure,' came his quick reply. 'How many bags?'

'Ready to go, Diana?' I ask.

'Yes,' she replies, and gets up from her chair. We thank everyone at the church and say our goodbyes.

At home, Diana settles into her chair while I unpack the shopping. I'm halfway through painting the spare room, and want to put on another coat of paint before lunch. 'Are you in any hurry for lunch, Diana?' I call.

'None at all,' she says. 'I had quite a substantial morning tea.'

I place the bluetooth speaker in the hall so that we can both hear it, and put on a podcast. The morning rolls into the afternoon as the heat slowly builds and Diana dozes in her chair. I go outside to wash the paintbrush at the corner tap in the front yard.

'Hello, Tony,' someone calls out.

I look up and it's Shawn. With him are Cheyenne and Jaydon and another person. It takes me a few moments to realise it's Smiley from Dajarra, who was part of the rescue mission when I was stuck out bush.

'What are you doing here?' I ask.

'I'm Cheyenne's aunty,' Smiley replies.

I look to Cheyenne. 'You should come to the meeting next week, then?' Members of Smiley's, and by extension Cheyenne's, family have been in discussions with me about a new native title claim to the south.

'Nah. Gotta look after bub,' Cheyenne replies. 'Best leave it to the aunties.'

'Is this where you live?' Smiley asks.

'Yes. With Beck's mum,' I reply. 'Beck's away but she flies back tonight. You around tomorrow?'

'Head back to Dajarra this afternoon.'

'Call in next time,' I tell her. I can see that Jaydon's getting grisly and pulling at his dad's hand. 'You better keep moving.'

We say goodbye, and I go back into the house and start rustling up some lunch. I tell Diana about seeing Smiley.

'It's so different to Melbourne. I never bump into anybody I work with there, unless it's at a meeting. It's always about work business. Here it feels more normal. I like it.'

'I'm pleased for you,' says Diana.

I serve up lunch.

'That's an unusual name,' Diana says a few moments later.

'What is?' I ask.

'Smiley.'

I laugh. 'That's not her real name. That's just what everyone calls her.' I tell Diana her full name.

'I taught someone with that name in Cloncurry. An Aboriginal boy. I remember he was a very good student. He knew the names of all the plants and animals.'

Diana's memory impresses me – that must have been seventy years ago, before she met Ted. 'I'll ask if they're related next time I see her. Perhaps we can get her over. I'm sure she'd like to see Beck again. She's really friendly.'

'Hence the name!' says Diana.

After lunch, I finish the spare room, make sure the house is really tidy and wrap the ukulele I bought online for Beck.

Standing on the back landing, I see a Qantas jet flying low along the eastern side of town, just above the range. 'That's her plane, I reckon,' I call out to Diana, who is freshly showered and changed, and back in her chair. 'I'll be back soon.'

'I'll set the table,' Diana announces.

I know Diana will get out the good tablecloth and the good crockery and cutlery. She may not be a big fan of 'a selection of salads', but she's pleased her baby will soon be home, and she wants to make a fuss.

9

PUTTING DOWN PINEAPPLES

Rebecca

Lucille and I listen to music on the radio as we drive along Lygon Street towards Allie's house. It's a crisp autumn day and the sun streams through the car windows. I feel cosy sitting in the passenger seat, listening to the music. This is my favourite time of year in Melbourne.

I can hear a ukulele in the song that's playing. I pretend to hold my ukulele and practice the strumming pattern I'm trying to get the hang of. I have been watching online ukulele tutorials. I hold my index finger and thumb together. I think about my index nail hitting the string on the strum down and the pad on the top of my thumb hitting it on the way up. I practise the pattern: down, down, up, up, down, up, down.

Ash, a musician from Mum's church, recently gave me a very short strumming lesson. He told me to focus on moving my wrist rather than my hand when I strum, and suggested I try to relax more. I know he's right. I am keen but impatient, and hold myself tightly when I play. For a few days after the lesson I did feel an improvement. I managed to coordinate all the parts: the strumming pattern, the notes, my wrist and the singing.

I've taken to practising and playing on Friday nights. Mum and Tony sit on the verandah with me after dinner and listen as I play and sing. They're a good audience, singing along and clapping after each effort.

I'm currently learning 'Don't Pull Your Love' by Hamilton, Joe Frank & Reynolds, an old hit from the early 1970s. I recently heard it on the radio and remembered how much I'd loved it as a kid. I looked it up online and found that the ukulele chords were quite simple. What I lack in skill I make up for in enthusiasm.

'I'm amazed how quickly you've picked it up, Beck,' Mum said.

I didn't tell her, but the thing with the uke is that you can get to a level of basic competency quite quickly. I also know that if I don't do a bit more practice, I won't be able to advance beyond the three songs I can currently play. Along with 'Don't Pull Your Love', I've been plucking out 'Over the Rainbow', a uke classic, and – especially for Mum – 'It's Only a Paper Moon'.

I had thought about bringing the uke with me on this trip so I could keep practising, but decided against it. I'm only in Melbourne for a few days and thought it'd be a bit gammon to bring it along. I have to confess that I liked the idea of accessorising with it. I've always wanted to experience the particular cool that comes with carrying an instrument through an airport.

Lucille looks over and asks me what I'm doing. I tell her that I'm practising strumming on my air ukulele.

'Haven't you and Dad joined a uke group?' she asks.

'Handbells group,' I say.

'Oh yeah, that's right. Is that like town criers?'

I shake my head and laugh. 'The bells are shaped like the ones the town crier uses except there are heaps of them, from small to large, and they correlate to the notes on the piano. You lay them out on the table in the same order as the keys, with white on one line and black placed above them, and when you have to play a note you pick up the corresponding bell.'

'Do you just play one note?'

'Usually each player has a few bells that they play throughout a piece of music. You pick one up and ring it, then put it down and then get another one. Sometimes you have to have a bell in each hand and get ready to ring and then change.'

'Sounds hectic,' says Lucille.

'It is!'

'Have you played a gig yet?' she asks.

'Yep. We played two songs at the recent eisteddfod.'

'Did you win?'

'Yep, first prize in the community group section. You should have seen Grandma – she was so proud.'

'Classic!' says Lucille.

I neglect to add that we were the only entrants in our category. Some details just ruin a good story.

Lucille turns onto Argyle Street and parks. Before getting out of the car, she asks, 'Are you nervous?'

'A bit,' I say, 'but it's more excitement than nerves. How about you?'

'Same.'

We get out of the car and cross the street. Lucille knocks on the door and we stand and wait. I step back and look up at the house. It's an old but beautiful terrace, and appears to be in very good condition. I'm a bit surprised, as I'd thought that share houses in Carlton were next to extinct.

A young woman opens the door and invites us in. She smiles

and tells us Allie is out the back. We walk down the hall, past bikes, boxes and other bits and pieces, through the galley-style kitchen and out to the back area. There are some old chairs and couches, neglected-looking plants, milk crates serving as tables, and overflowing ashtrays. I am immediately propelled back thirty years to the share houses I lived in.

Allie jumps up to greet us. 'Beck!' she says, and wraps her arms around me in a bear hug. She greets Lucille with the same warmth. 'Love your dress,' she says to me.

'Thank you! It was my mum's.'

'Oh wow, that's so cool!'

I smile and nod. It is cool. I have found a few favourite dresses of Mum's from the 1970s and have started to wear them. Most are ones she made. Today's number is a light grey polished-cotton three-panelled shift. It has yellow and orange flowers on it and a small collar that ties at the front with a bow.

'I can't believe we can both wear the same dresses,' Mum had exclaimed. 'I thought I was a very different shape from you at the same age.'

I understand what she's saying: Mum always thought she was fat. As a young woman Mum had been very slight, but as she aged her shape changed and she didn't like it. She was someone who placed an inordinate amount of importance on size and shape. She held a view – often unspoken, but obvious in the things she said and did – that being slim was more appealing in every sense. To her, being larger-bodied meant you were greedy, lazy and lacking in self-care.

As she got bigger, Mum fought with her body. She berated herself, and often restricted food and then overate. It was difficult because she was an excellent cook and loved good food. For years she went to Weight Watchers. Initially she would lose weight, but then she'd put it all back on, plus more. Back then no one spoke about one's relationships with body, food or behaviour. It was all very superficial.

The thing Mum hated most at Weight Watchers was the 'pig pen'. If it were discovered, at the weekly weigh-in, that you had put on weight, you would be put into the pig pen. It was an actual toddlers' playpen, and all the women inside the pen had to repeat: 'Piggy, piggy, piggy me, eating all that I can see.' On weigh-in days Mum would starve herself, go to Weight Watchers, do the weigh-in and then rush home after the meeting and tuck into the contents of the fridge.

'Did you have to go into the pig pen tonight, Mum?' we'd ask when she got home.

Thankfully, as she moved into her seventies, she stopped the battle and found comfort in her body, and was able to accept it and relax.

Allie puts out her cigarette in the ashtray. 'Ready?'

Lucille and I nod.

'Okay, let's go upstairs,' she says.

Allie indicates for Lucille and me to sit. Lucille sits on the bed, kicks her boots off and stretches out. She chats with Allie as she gets things ready. They talk about friends they have in common, and laugh about this and that.

I'm not sure where to sit and so remain standing. I look around the room. It's airy and sparsely furnished. The window is open and I can see the roof outside. There are a couple of empty beer bottles and an ashtray propped up against one of the beams. I imagine climbing through the window onto the roof and watching the sun set over the city.

Allie sits on a stool and pushes a chair out from the desk for me. 'So you're first?' she says to me, as she pulls on a pair of black latex gloves.

I look at Lu and she nods, so I nod.

Allie smiles and takes a small plastic bag from the desk and opens it. She takes out a stencil of a pineapple and gives it to me to look at. It's about five centimetres long and two wide. Lucille's boyfriend Max has drawn it from a suggestion I gave him. I like it. I nod and hand it back.

My arm lies along the armrest of my chair. Allie presses the tattoo stencil onto the underside of my lower right arm. She fills a small plastic cup with dark blue ink, puts a blob of moisturiser on the bottom of the cup and then sticks it to my lower arm. She takes a long, sharp needle out of a sterilised pack and dabs it in the ink.

'It won't hurt for the first few minutes,' she tells me.

I nod.

'But after that it probably will.'

I nod again.

Allie begins. She's right – the first few pricks don't hurt. 'Is this your first tatt?' she asks.

I nod.

'Does Grandma know?' asks Lu from the bed.

I shake my head.

'Really?' she asks.

I nod.

'Ooh!' she laughs. 'Bad Mom!' she says, putting on an American accent.

I laugh too.

'What will she say?' asks Lu.

'She always says, "*I loathe tattoos,*"' I say, imitating my mother's voice.

Lu laughs. 'But all the Mount Isa grandkids have them. Isn't she used to them by now?'

'Yeah, but you know, it's sort of become her thing to shake her head at tatts. "*Makes you look like you've been involved in some kind of illegal activity.*"'

We all laugh.

After the first few minutes, my arm does start to hurt. I focus on my breathing. I watch Allie's steady hands move down my arm as she inks the outline of the pineapple.

'Why now?' she asks.

It's a good question and I think for a moment.

'I feel as though I've reached an age where I'm completely comfortable with who I am,' I say at last. 'I told the girls years ago that we would get matching tatts, so here we are!'

'And Georgie?' Allie asks.

'She was a bit naughty,' I say.

'Like you, Mum,' Lucille breaks in.

I laugh. 'She got hers done on her wrist in a bar in New York without us.'

Lu sticks up for her sister: 'She says she didn't realise we were all going to get them done together!'

I smile and nod. We both know Georgie got it done first because she is impetuous, but it's no big deal. If I was in a bar in New York and there was a tattoo artist there who was charging five dollars a go, then I'd be thinking, 'What will I get done?' too.

Allie continues to work the needle across my arm. Each jab is like a purposeful pinprick – you notice it, but it's nothing to be alarmed by. Allie is a 'stick and poke' tattoo artist. This means she does all her tattoos by hand. She doesn't use a tattoo gun.

I look down. She's finished the outline of the pineapple.

'Looks good, hey?' she asks.

I smile and nod.

Allie starts working on the inside detail. 'Do you grow pineapples where you live in Queensland?' she asks.

'I do,' I say, 'but it's not the norm. Pineapples grow better in places like Cairns, where it's hot and wet, but I'm managing to keep mine alive in Mount Isa.'

'How many do you have now?' asks Lu.

Initially I had three growing in pots and a few in the cycad garden beside the back steps. But now I've started to plant more at the end of the backyard. 'I've lost count,' I say.

'How long before they fruit?' asks Allie.

'About five years.'

'Five years!' says Allie. 'And are you going to stay there until they do?'

'Maybe,' I shrug.

Lu raises her eyebrows but says nothing.

'But we're not getting the pineapple as a tatt because I grow them,' I say to Allie.

'Mum's the Pineapple Princess,' says Lu.

Allie looks at me questioningly.

I shrug and smile. 'She was a comedy character I used to do in Daylesford in my late thirties. She was a provincial and slightly faded glamorous Queenslander, who was crowned the Pineapple Princess at a fictitious festival in Bundaberg in the late 1970s.'

'Oh yeah,' says Allie.

'Her claims to fame were her open mind, excellent common sense and the ability to prepare the Pineapple Princess dish live on stage while drinking a few shots of rum and singing "Beautiful Queensland".'

'What's the Pineapple Princess dish?' asks Allie.

'Well, Allie, it's actually a bit of a party pleaser! Chunks of cheese and cabana are stuck on a toothpick and topped off with a glacé cherry. The loaded toothpicks are then stuck into the diamond pattern on the pineapple, and the whole ensemble becomes a stunning table centrepiece. The beauty of the dish is its versatility – perfect for the cocktail hour, afternoon barbecue or when guests turn up unannounced.'

Allie laughs.

'In Daylesford people started to call me the Pineapple Princess, and then the pineapple gifts started. Initially it was a few items here and there – a tea towel, a set of earrings – but soon it spread to everyone in my life. I have heaps of pineapple things that people have given me – clothes, pictures, towels, jewellery, art, crockery, lamps, ornaments, socks, underwear … it's incredible how many pineapple items there are out there.'

'And now a piney tatt,' adds Lu.

'Yep,' I laugh.

'So that means Lu and Georgie are Pineapple Princesses by birthright?' Allie asks.

'Absolutely!'

We laugh, and then the room goes quiet. Allie's head is very close to my arm. I can see the pulse in her temples and the hair follicles on the top of her head and the side of her face. I wonder whether it would hurt to pluck out one of those hairs. Mum gets me to pluck the stray hairs from her chin and eyebrows. They are quite fine, but she winces with each pulled hair. Sometimes I'm careless with the tweezers and catch small bits of skin in the pincers and yank that away too. This causes Mum to yelp. She's on blood-thinning medication so there's often a lot of blood, even though the accidental snips are tiny.

As well as plucking, I do Mum's manicures and pedicures. She used to go to a chiropodist to get her feet done, and the granddaughters have at times also had to do it, but she's now handed the honour to me. I don't mind. I like feet.

Grooming night has become a bit of an event. We do it when Tony is not there. First, I do Mum's plucking, and then we set up for the pedicure. A few years ago one of the granddaughters gave

Mum a home pedicure spa tub. It's a small basin that you fill with water, then you turn on a switch and the water heats up. I add bath salts, and when it's warm enough Mum puts her feet in. Then I turn on the small jets. Mum always closes her eyes and leans back.

After the spa I dry her feet and use a pumice stone to remove the softened dry skin. Then I begin on her toenails. I've discovered that, as we get older, the toenail almost seems to grow into the skin. I use a blunt instrument to get any dirt out from under the toenail, and to lift it up slightly so I can get the clippers in position. Occasionally, I've snipped Mum's skin. I hate it when I do this. When I've finished clipping, I massage her feet and cover them in soft socks.

What I would really like to do is give Mum a full massage. She loves me rubbing moisturiser into her hands, arms, legs and face.

'We should book you in for a massage, Mum,' I said one time.

'No thanks,' she replied.

'You'd love it!'

'I'm not taking my clothes off for a stranger.'

'They're not strangers – they're just friends you haven't met yet!'

Mum snorted.

'When Georgina and Lucille were little, I would massage them on the kitchen table,' I told her.

'I'm not getting up on the table!' said Mum.

'But I've already hired a hoist,' I joked. 'And I've told them you'll be naked.'

Mum looked at me, eyes and mouth agog, and then burst out laughing.

Allie has completed the front part of the tattoo, and has started on the diamond shapes that make up the body of the pineapple. 'How long are you going to stay in the Isa for, Beck?' she asks.

Lucille rolls over on the bed and looks at me. 'Yeah, Mum, how long are you going to stay in the Isa?'

'As long as it takes,' I say.

'As long as it takes for your mum to die?' Allie asks.

I nod.

'So it could be soon or it could be years?' she says.

I nod.

'You must like it,' she says.

'I do,' I say.

'What do you like best?' she asks.

This is another good question. 'I like caring for Mum, and I like the big wide-open sky. I like the colour of the earth, and even though it is a big, dirty mining town, I know it like the back of my hand and it's always felt like home. I like that.'

'I get that,' she says.

I look over at Lucille. She nods and smiles. The girls get it too. They know they are deeply loved, and that they're our number one people, but Mum and the Mount Isa family are right up there too.

'It's a good thing that you're doing,' Allie says.

'Thanks,' I say. 'I think so too.'

Allie turns to Lucille. 'Are you gunna do that for Beck when she's old, Lu?'

'Georgie said she would do it,' Lu replies.

I laugh.

'No, seriously,' says Lu, 'we've already got you and Dad booked into a nursing home.'

We all laugh, but I make a mental note that nothing has changed from our conversation of over a year ago.

I don't say anything for a moment. Of course this question has crossed my mind in the last sixteen months. Is part of what Tony and I doing also about setting a good example for our children?

Is what we are doing for Mum what we want our children to do for us?

'The thing with Mum,' I say, 'was that she didn't ever want to talk about, or make plans for, when she would be too old to look after herself. She maintained active avoidance and denial until there was no other option. Hopefully Tony and I won't do that.'

'Even if you do,' says Lu, 'Georgie and I will still look after you.'

My heart skips a beat. I would never want to force my children into having to do this for me, but it is good to know that they have this sense of empathy and loyalty.

'But I get first pick of the things in your wardrobe,' Lu adds.

I shrug and laugh. Everything comes at a price. I've got no idea what the future might bring, but I do make a pledge to myself that I will try to be open and engaged in taking responsibility for my ageing.

Allie sits back and gestures to the finished tattoo. I stare at it for quite a while without saying anything. It suddenly dawns on me that it is permanent.

'Do you like it?' she asks.

'You bet I do!' I say.

'Pineapples forever,' says Allie.

I nod and smile. 'Yeah, pineapples forever!'

10

STUMBLE

Tony

I'm on the early Monday-morning water taxi from Stradbroke Island to the mainland. I've done this journey a couple of times before, years ago when I used to live in Brisbane – before Beck, before kids. It's stunningly beautiful, and back then I would spend the journey imagining an island life, going to work each morning across the bay with the high-school kids and commuters. But today I'm too anxious to indulge this fantasy. I'm not sure if I'll have a job by the end of the week.

I've spent the weekend with our good friend Judy, who is holidaying on the island, and today I'm returning to Brisbane for work. I'm meant to be going to a two-day strategic planning workshop with my colleagues. It was my idea to have the workshop, and the CEO, Warren, was quick to get on board with it. But now he is angry with me, and has directed me not to attend.

It all fell apart last Friday when I was negotiating my next one-year contract. Warren thought I was being unreasonable and shut down discussions.

I ring my direct boss as the boat pulls up alongside the jetty. He tells me the CEO's still angry and suggests I work from the Brisbane office until my flight back to Mount Isa in two days' time. 'We can sort it out later,' he says.

This doesn't fill me with confidence. I'm embarrassed by the misunderstanding and the subsequent falling-out. Until now, my relationship with Warren has been good and I rated him highly. I'm also upset by the worry the matter is causing Beck and Diana. They are, first and foremost, worried for me, but I know that within that worry is the question of whether we can remain in Mount Isa if I lose my job. The whole project is in jeopardy.

Eventually, I return to Mount Isa, and over the course of the following week I'm told that I will be, despite the falling-out, offered another contract on largely unchanged terms. Before signing it, I insist on a telephone meeting with Warren. I want to know if I can have a sensible conversation with him, and if he'll offer an explanation for his behaviour. He's unavailable to meet with me for over a week, but eventually we talk. After explaining the reasons for his anger, he offers me an apology. I'm not entirely convinced, but for the sake of keeping my job and being able to stay in Mount Isa, I accept it. Still upset, I hang up. I'm unsure how long I'm going to last.

A few hours later Beck calls to tell me our dinner plans that night with friends have fallen through. It was, in fact, our first non-family invitation since moving here, and coincides with the one-year anniversary of our arrival. But I'm not in a going-out mood anyway, and we realise it would be better to celebrate the anniversary at home with Diana. I buy some fish from the iceworks and Beck puts a bottle of champagne in the fridge. When I get home from work we have a beer under the house. The rocky hills are afire with the setting sun.

'I don't think he gets it,' I tell Beck.

'Gets what?' Beck asks.

'Gets that his behaviour has a strong impact on people. I think he genuinely believes it's all sorted, and we'll go back to business as usual.'

'What do you want to do?' Beck asks. 'Do you need to go back to your old job in Melbourne?'

'What I want to do and need to do are two separate things. I want to tell Warren to shove it, but I need to let it go. I need to get on with the job and get on with life here.'

Beck takes my hand, leans in and kisses me gently on the lips. 'Thank you.'

By now it's dark and we head upstairs to cook our fish and chips. After dinner we take our champagne outside onto the verandah. It's still very hot. I put on some Ella Fitzgerald and for a while we sit in silence, until Beck starts to softly sing 'It's Only a Paper Moon'. After a while Diana and I join in, at first tentatively and then with more confidence. For the next hour the three of us sing, tap and hum along to the music.

It's Saturday night, and we've just finished dinner. Beck and Diana start a game of Upwords while I go outside to move the sprinklers. By the time I come back up the stairs, Beck and Diana have slipped into roleplay.

Beck is an Irish character called Kathleen. 'Well, you wouldn't be trying to cheat on me, now, Ma?'

Diana laughs and plays along. 'I don't need to cheat to win.'

She's out of practice and her accent's not as good as Beck's, but the two of them become hysterical. I can't help but smile as I wash up.

It seems like a veil has been lifted from Beck. She's a happy person by nature, but at times self-doubt and worry have brought her low. But here, under the western sun, in her childhood home, she's consistently buoyant.

'Perhaps Kathleen and her cheating friend could help me with the dishes,' I suggest from the sink.

'You've got to be feckin' kidding,' Beck says. 'That's what you're here for, boyo. You're of no other use to us.'

'Yeah, what she says,' echoes Diana.

I finish the dishes on my own and go to the lounge to read my book, and Beck and Diana continue to play. Beck leads for most of the game, but Diana comes home strongly and wins.

It's still early, and Beck suggests we go to The Shack. The Shack is the fortnightly open-mic night run by the local folk club. I'm ambivalent. We've been three or four times over the last twelve months, and while I enjoy going to an extent, I find it hard to fully embrace. This makes me feel churlish. What's better than people having fun and being creative, making music? And I come from a musical family, so you'd think I'd support it. But the performers aren't very good, I tell myself, so why bother? They're not my brother, sister, niece or nephew. They're not rising stars on the scene in Melbourne. I worry that my reluctance is snobbish.

I know Beck's keen to get out of the house and check out what's going on, and it's not as if we have many other options. 'Okay, I'm in,' I tell her.

It's still stinking hot as we walk along the track by the side of the river. The glowing mine is straight ahead of us, and looks forbidding as it hums and shimmers beneath a haze of heat and dust. We walk past Beck's old primary school, and she points to a dark gully around the back. 'That's where we did Aboriginal culture in Grade Four or Five. Over a week we built a gunya out of bark and sticks, and then on the last day the teacher handed out lolly grubs – "bush tucker," he said. And that was it – the sixty-thousand-year history of this country in one week.'

We continue walking. I try to imagine Beck as a kid running around the schoolyard and down in the dry creek bed with her classmates. Sweaty and excitable.

Our friend Annette and her daughter Misha are on stage when we arrive. They sound good together. The place is three-quarters full and we find a table near one of the big oscillating fans bracketed to the wall. It's an open-air venue but the heat lies heavy. I go to the bar and buy two XXXX Golds – no tickets required here.

The place fills up quickly with large groups of half-cut young miners with nowhere else to go. The mother–daughter duo is replaced by a group of schoolteachers of varying ability. Their enthusiasm helps cover the gaps, and they get a good response from the crowd.

Next up is a thin man in his fifties. He's wearing harem pants, a cotton vest and an old leather hat and sandals, and he's adorned with feathers and bells. I ask Rob, who I know from writers' group, who this is. 'Feather Foot,' he tells me with a grin.

Feather Foot starts in on a turgid set of ballads that ramble and blend into each other. Rob says that Feather Foot comes and goes from the town, never staying more than a couple of months, but that on his last appearance at The Shack he was hustled off the stage when he started on a racist and anti-immigrant rant. I suspect there'd be a lot of people here who'd have sympathy for those views, but The Shack is clearly a politically neutral zone. Thankfully, tonight he sticks to singing (poorly, mind you) and eventually exits the stage, much to everyone's relief.

Three men with guitars follow. They're also from the folk realm, but more colonial-era sea shanties. They seem to be enjoying themselves in an earnest kind of way, but none of them can sing and all three guitars sound the same (as do the songs). I'm profoundly bored. I turn to Beck, hopeful that she wants to go home, but she's talking to Annette and I know there's no chance.

I refocus on the men on stage. At first I admire their gumption to get up and have a go, but as their interminable set grinds on, my admiration turns to irritation. What makes them think they have the right to subject us to this? My guitar mastery extended to long Eric Bogle ballads, which I thought sounded great. No one else did, and soon I stopped playing. Has someone not similarly enlightened these fellas? For fear of being a curmudgeon, I keep my counsel.

The place continues to fill, and the crowd, largely indifferent to the drone from the stage, is getting rowdier. After what seems like an age the three balladeers finish, to desultory applause. Next up is a five-piece soul outfit. Now we're talking. They open with a punchy Stevie Wonder number, and immediately there's a crowd up and dancing. The musicians have quickly got 'into the zone'. I feel a flush of jealousy at the sheer joy that must bring. I wish I'd pushed past the ballads. I wish I'd responded to the urgings of my ancient trumpet teacher at school to practise, and not succumbed to teenage laziness. I swallow my regrets with a second XXXX Gold.

Too quickly the soul band get through their allotted time and make way for another five-piece band. At first this band also sounds promising – tight and loud, and the audience loves them. The lead singer tells us after the first song that he's just come back from a tour of Afghanistan, singing for the troops. He punches his fist into the air and launches into 'Khe Sanh'.

I like 'Khe Sanh' but this guy's swagger is making me uncomfortable. He's short and sneery, and exudes superiority and aggression. It doesn't seem to bother the others, who all join in as he claps his hands above his head and cheer raucously at the end of each song.

After four songs I turn to Beck pleadingly: 'Can we go?'

Mercifully, she nods her assent.

As we walk home we hear the singer's voice float across the dry riverbed above the tinkle of glass and laughter. 'This next one's for our boys still over there …'

The following day rolls along easily. I have a couple of long phone conversations with friends and family down south. The Sunday phone calls have become a lifesaver. Once I would spend Sunday afternoons writing letters – I remember my mum doing that when I was a child – but now it's emails and phone calls.

The calls connect me with the outside world and allow me to relax and accept the isolation of this place. Once the edge comes off the heat, I decide to dig some holes for the new plants Beck insisted we buy on the way home from yoga.

'Don't you think we have enough?' I had asked.

We've already planted at least thirty new trees and bushes, mainly natives – not that all have survived in the rocky soil and heat. Their maintenance, especially the watering, is already a burden.

'I want to plant out the whole yard,' Beck said. 'Get rid of the lawn eventually.'

Inwardly, I had groaned. Not just at the cost of the new plants and the work involved, but at what I suspect is her real motivation. Beck, consciously or unconsciously, is re-establishing her connection to Mount Isa. As each plant throws roots that penetrate the hard soil, so too are we pushing through the layers of resistance felt in any new town. With every plant that takes hold and grows, our commitment deepens. With each new hole I dig, it will become harder to leave.

But whatever her motivation, I don't actually mind. I like the physicality of the digging. I like seeing things take root and grow against the odds. And especially I like seeing Beck so happy.

171

The heat is unrelenting. It's Easter and still it's hot – forty degrees hot. Diana, who rarely complains, tells me she doesn't want to live through another summer. It's hard not to think that would be the best option all round as I prepare to take off for Melbourne to visit the girls and to house-hunt.

Georgina and Lucille, who have been living in our rented townhouse in Clifton Hill, have decided it's time for them to move into share houses. 'We're sick of looking after your house and living amongst your ratty furniture and tacky knick-knacks,' they announce. 'We're sick of doing you a favour.'

Oh, how the narrative has changed! Fifteen months ago it was us doing them a favour. Affording them (and the couch surfers) the comfort and luxury of subsidised inner-city living in a fully furnished house, with a car, while they finish their degrees and cavort around the world on exchanges and internships. Suddenly they're the ones doing us a favour, forced to remain at home and denied the opportunity to live with friends and become independent.

It's hard to tell how much of this narrative the girls actually believe. Regardless, we decide that, come August, when our lease expires, we won't renew, and the girls agree to stay on until then. That means, though, that we have to decide what to do with a house full of furniture while we remain in Mount Isa. I investigate storage options and they're prohibitively expensive, especially given we have no idea how long it will be before we come back – if we ever do.

We give serious consideration to buying a place in Murwillumbah. Our good friends Pete and Dave live there, and they tell us it'll be the next place to take off. We like northern New South Wales, and the idea of being close to the coast. But the thought of setting up somewhere new whenever Diana dies, and still being so far away from the kids, holds us back.

We start looking in Daylesford, a place we know well, only a stone's throw from Melbourne. Over Easter I find a place that's just a street away from where we used to live. I send Beck the link and she gives her nod of approval – it's structurally sound, centrally heated, and has a big shed to store our furniture – but a few days later she emails me again:

> I know this sounds completely nuts – but I really like it here. I feel very content of late. I love my work and feel as though there are lots of opportunities here. The issue is the long, hot summer and the distance away from all our mates.

Despite Beck's hesitation, we decide to buy the Daylesford place. It satisfies our need to be tethered somewhere. We discuss what we could do to the house when we live there – open up the back and build a pizza oven, turn the shed into a bungalow, render the ugly bricks, plant out the front yard – but we know that it's unlikely we ever will. Still, the fantasy allows us to continue to live in Mount Isa indefinitely, without the disquieting sense of floating free that keeps us awake at night.

I pick up the consultant anthropologist and barrister from the airport, and we head straight to Camooweal, where we're staying the night on our way to the Aboriginal community of Alpurrurulam, just over the border in the Northern Territory. The consultants have been engaged to assist with a native title matter that has become particularly fraught.

I'm pleased to be getting out of town and out of the office. Over the last couple of weeks my relationship with head office has deteriorated further, and whatever sense of refreshment and resolve

I brought back from my three weeks in Melbourne has completely dissipated. I know I have to start looking for other work in Mount Isa, and potentially elsewhere.

We rise early the next day, and head south across the southern Barkly Tableland. We enter a vast Mitchell grass plain. I feel like we're bouncing along the top of the world, with the country dipping away in every direction. After a couple of hours we re-enter low, scrubby woodland, and eventually we cross the Georgina River at a small ford. This is the river our daughter Georgina was named after.

Beck's dad, Ted, spent a lot of time fishing along this river, which starts north of here on the edge of the gulf and runs south through the Channel Country, and, when flooding, merges with the Diamantina before flowing on to Lake Eyre in South Australia. I'm in awe of the magnitude of this drainage system, which covers one-fifth of the continent. Just up from the crossing is a large billabong called Lake Nash, from which the massive surrounding station takes its name. In the 1980s, four square kilometres of scrubby bush, well away from the waterhole, were excised from the station to create the Aboriginal town of Alpurrurulum.

The three of us spend a couple of days there, talking to people about how they are linked to country just across the border back in Queensland. Native title is a long-winded business, and these people have been talking about it for years to various lawyers and anthropologists, but despite their frustrations and initial distrust, by the end of our last day there's a large crowd sitting around us under the shade of the basketball court, talking freely about their connections to country.

We decide to detour via Urandangie on the way back to Mount Isa. We call in at the pub for a lemon squash, and then make our way to Marmanya, a small outstation on the edge of town. Marmanya was set up as a model community back in the early 1990s, with architecturally designed state-of-the-art houses. Over time it fell into severe disrepair, and the corporation established to run it became defunct and failed to pay rates for years.

When I first moved to Mount Isa, there was a strong desire by many in the community to get the place up and running again, but negotiations with the titles office and the council have stalled. This hasn't stopped one family from moving back in, and repairing some of the houses and planting a garden. I'm heartened by the agency and industry this family has displayed, not waiting for the turgid bureaucratic wheels to roll.

I drop the consultants at their motel and head home. Beck and Diana are watching *Letters and Numbers*. I dump my gear and, it being an even day, go outside with a beer in hand and water the garden. The trip has been interesting and profoundly satisfying. I feel the best I have in weeks.

11

THIS IS LIVING

Rebecca

At lunch Mum asks, 'Did you pick up my medication?'

'Nah, I couldn't be bovvered,' I say.

Mum laughs, and says with a nasal drawl, 'Yeah, couldn't be bovvered.'

We both giggle. This is one of our favourite little expressions.

Years ago I was facilitating a series of drama workshops for a group of young women in Wynnum, in Brisbane. One week, only half the women turned up. I was surprised, as the workshops had, up until then, been very well attended.

'Where are the others today?' I asked one of the women.

'I was talkin' to 'em,' she said, 'and they said they couldn't be bovvered comin'.'

I laughed. 'Fair enough!'

I totally got it – some days you just can't be bothered! And there's no point in lying or calling it anything else. Apathy deserves its time in the sun. I'd told Mum what the young woman had said and she'd loved it.

'I did try to go to the chemist before coming home for lunch,' I tell Mum, 'but downtown was so crowded and I couldn't get a park.'

'The grey nomads are in town for Mardi Gras and the rodeo,' Mum says. 'I saw all the campervans when I was on the bus.'

'Yep,' I say, 'the town is awash with grey nomads and ringers.'

'Seen any buckle bunnies?' says Mum.

'Oh, Mum, don't say that!' I say.

'Why not?' she asks. 'Tony calls you one.'

I cringe a bit. 'He's being ironic!' I protest.

Mum is right – Tony does call me a buckle bunny. I have a wardrobe full of western clothes – shirts, belts, hats, boots – and I love a bit of rodeo sparkle on my belt buckles and jeans. I'm definitely a try-hard cowgirl, but I am not a buckle bunny.

'It's a derogatory term,' I tell Mum. 'It's used as a slur to describe women who supposedly hang around rodeo grounds trying to pick up rodeo champions. They usually wear tiny denim cut-off shorts with big belts, western shirts tied at the front, high-heeled boots and lots of sparkle and bling.'

'Are you going to wear that on the Mardi Gras float?' Mum asks.

'No, of course not! We're all wearing our Headspace work shirts!'

'That's not much fun,' says Mum.

She's right – it's not much fun. I had hoped we might be wearing costumes, or at least dressing up, but ultimately I don't mind what I have to wear. In all the years I have been associated with Mount Isa I've never been on a Mardi Gras float, so I'm pretty stoked to be getting a chance at last.

The Mardi Gras is an annual Mount Isa night-time community parade. It marks the start of the three-day rodeo. Anyone can enter a float, and people go to great lengths to decorate them. There's good prize money up for grabs for the best efforts. It's a lively event. Everyone comes out in their hats and chequered shirts and lines the main streets to watch. There's food, drink and live music, and after the parade people wander down to the rodeo grounds to watch the bull riding championships or head to Fred Brophy's boxing tent.

When I was a kid, Mum always made me a new cowgirl outfit for Mardi Gras and rodeo, and we all got new hats. We'd go out to the rodeo grounds as a family, watch the events and go on the rides in sideshow alley. It was one of the few events that Dad didn't drink at. David would always go in the calf-riding event, which was pretty exciting.

I love the energy the rodeo brings to town, but I hate the cruelty to the animals. As a kid, I hated seeing horses break their legs. A horse would fall and someone would come into the main arena with a gun and shoot it. A crane with a harness would then be rolled out and the horse would be carted away. I remember being terrified watching the bronco events for fear that a horse would get injured. I still hate the way animals are treated in rodeos – the use of spurs, flank straps and electronic prodders. I love events like the barrel races that show the skill of both human and horse. I'd be happy with a rodeo of just that, but I know I'd be laughed out of town if I suggested it. The rodeo is a huge tourist attraction and plays a big role in maintaining Mount Isa's reputation as a frontier settlement. But for many locals the events are irrelevant and it's just an excuse for a three-day piss-up.

'Are the buckle bunnies like groupies?' Mum asks.

'Yeah,' I say. 'I think *cowgirls* or *Rodeo Queen entrants* is probably the term you're looking for, Mum.'

'No,' says Mum, 'the term I was looking for was definitely buckle bunny!'

I laugh and go back to my lunch.

'Did you ever want to be a Rodeo Queen entrant?' Mum asks.

'No,' I say.

'You were Miss Mount Isa High School,' she says.

I say nothing.

'Seems like a natural trajectory,' Mum presses.

'I didn't want to be a Rodeo Queen, Mum!'

'You could have been driven down the main street draped across the front of a new Holden,' she says, 'wearing an evening gown.'

'Mum!'

'What?'

'I didn't want to be a Rodeo Queen!'

'What about the Charity Queen?'

'Stop it!'

'You like doing good in the community. You could have raised money for Headcase.'

'It's Headspace, Mum, Head*space*!'

'Oh yes, Headspace.'

'It didn't exist back then.'

'That's a pity. You could have made a lot of money for them. The queens raise a lot of money for charity.'

Some days I wonder if Mum's medication is making her too happy.

'Your grandmother used to ride in rodeos,' Mum says.

'When?'

'When she was young. She was an excellent rider, and loved the rodeo events.'

'Why have you never told me this before?'

'I only thought of it now.'

I look at Mum and realise that her response is genuine. Our family have been to hundreds of rodeos, and this is the first time I've ever heard this fact about my grandmother. Life with Mum sometimes feels like a slow-reveal soap opera. With each episode another piece of information is revealed, allowing the characters to become a fraction more rounded.

'Was she ever a Rodeo Queen?' I ask.

'Not that I know of!'

'A buckle bunny?'

Mum laughs. 'Don't be so ridiculous!'

We finish our lunch and have a quick game of cribbage.

As I leave to go back to work, Mum says, 'Don't forget my medication.'

'I won't,' I say. 'I'll go straight after work.'

'You better make it fast otherwise you'll miss *Letters and Numbers*,' she says.

'I'll be home in time. You better have the kettle on!'

'If I can be bovvered,' Mum says.

'What did your mum make for lunch today?' Jacquie, my boss at Headspace, asks when I return to the office.

'Vegetable and barley soup,' I reply.

'Yum!' she says.

'And I had fruitcake and a cup of tea for dessert.'

'I want that lunch!' she laughs. Some of the other staff in the office hear our conversation and laugh too.

'How's your mum?' asks Christina.

Christina is a colleague at work. We've become friends. She has an elderly father, and while he doesn't live with her in Mount Isa, she's acutely aware of all the vulnerabilities that come with old age. She often enquires about Mum.

'Perky,' I say.

Christina laughs. 'Any more falls?'

I nod. 'I was sitting down at Dinky's on Saturday afternoon, having a chat on the phone to a friend in Melbourne, and I heard a thud upstairs. My friend heard it too. I said goodbye really quickly, raced upstairs and found Mum on the kitchen floor.'

'Did you have to get the ambulance again?'

I shake my head. 'I thought I was going to have to. It took me ages to get her up. She doesn't have much strength in her arms or legs, and I'm not quite strong enough to lift her by myself. I did eventually get her up and into her chair, checked her for lumps, bumps or cuts and then gave her a bowl of ginger pudding and custard. Pretty soon she was right as rain!'

Christina laughs. 'Good thing you were home, though.'

'I know.'

'How's Tony?'

'Good,' I say.

'That's good. You two are doing such a great job,' she says.

I smile and say thanks, then head to my desk.

I'd like to tell Christina the truth. Things are not good with Tony, but I know he doesn't want me to talk about it. I've barely even spoken about it with Mum. She knows something is up and has asked me if Tony is okay, but I don't want to discuss it with her. I think if she knew she would fret and worry that Tony felt trapped because of her.

Tony was not himself on the weekend.

'Can you dig me some more big holes out the back, Tone?' I had asked. I wanted to buy a few more native plants and get them in while the weather was cool.

'Why are you buying more plants?' he asked in return.

'To plant,' I said. 'Why else would I be buying plants?'

I thought this was quite humorous, but Tony didn't smile.

'I think we've put enough plants in,' he said.

'I don't.'

Tony didn't say anything.

'I want to plant the back out more,' I continued.

'Why?'

'So it looks better, so it attracts more birds, so it's not an ugly dustbowl.'

Still Tony said nothing.

'Do you think I'm spending too much money on plants?' I asked.

'No,' he replied.

'Do you want me to dig the holes?'

'I can do it.'

'So what's the problem?'

'The plants take so much time to look after.'

'I'll look after them. You don't have to,' I said.

At first Tony didn't reply, then finally he said, 'I feel like you want to plant and grow more things and put down deeper roots, and I just don't know if I'm able to stay here.'

'I know,' I said.

I could think of nothing more to say. I wrapped my arms around his lean frame and burrowed into his familiarity.

It's true. I can feel myself putting down more and deeper roots.

Recently I said to my friend Jude, 'I feel so great. I think it must be all the sunlight and vitamin D out here. Releases all the endorphins.'

'It might be that you're living with and caring for your mum,' she said. 'That sort of loving has got to be good for the endorphins too.'

For a moment I did not speak. Jude's comment created an electrical charge and I knew she was right. Looking after Mum and creating this life out here has made me feel deeply content.

'Yeah,' I said. 'I agree.'

I had thought that taking the job at Headspace might cause strain at home but it's actually been the opposite. It's done us all the world of good. It's opened up other things for the three of us to talk about. Mum loves hearing about my work and the various projects and events that are happening through Headspace.

I don't think I wanted to acknowledge it, but I was isolated last year, and unsure how to fix it. Now I have work and people who are becoming friends, and my world has expanded.

But for Tony it's been the opposite. Over the last few months he has looked at jobs in a variety of places, and each time I've been supportive and open to what that might look like. At one point he contemplated a move to Cairns. The plan was that he would go and I would stay here, but at the last moment I told him I just couldn't do it. We'd made the move out here together, and I couldn't imagine it being just Mum and me. Of course we'd both be fine, but we'd both be worse off for it. I do want to dig more holes and plant more trees, but I don't want to do it without Tony. I don't know what the solution is.

I spend the rest of the afternoon doing research for my mental health project, and supervising my two social work students. It's been a number of years since I have supervised students and I'm enjoying it. I've never held any academic aspirations but I like working with students while they learn how to put their academic knowledge into practice. I feel like I'm 'back on the tools', and I love it.

I leave work on the dot of 5 pm and drive to the pharmacy. I hope there's no queue, and that Mum's medications are ready. I'm keen to get home; I know Mum will be waiting for me. I head inside, and before I can even check out the queue situation I see a man coming towards me. He's grinning from ear to ear. Oh no, I think.

'Becca Lister!' he calls out.

I smile and he strides up to me. I stretch my hand out before he gets close enough to hug me; he has the look of a hugger.

'Hey!' I say, all upbeat and perky.

'You look exactly the same!' he says. 'I'd recognise you anywhere!'

I just smile.

'Don't ya remember me?' he asks. His smile is so broad that I don't have the heart to tell him the truth. I tilt my head and narrow my eyes, and hope that I'm giving the impression of someone trying to conjure up when they last saw their good old pal.

'Grade 1, Barkly Highway Primary School!' he says.

You've got to be joking, I think. I stand with my mouth agape, unable to think of anything to say.

'Bruce!' he says. 'Bruce Barlow!'

'Bruce, right, of course!' I say.

'Remember me sister, Karen?' he asks.

'Yeah!' I say, but of course I have no idea who she is either.

'She's still a bitch,' he says.

I can't think of anything to say to this, but it doesn't matter. Bruce has the conversation in hand.

'I seen you were back in town,' he says.

I nod and smile.

'I seen ya down Kmart, and then in the paper for Headspace and that.'

I nod and smile.

'We didn't have nothing like that when we was kids, ay?'

'Nope,' I say. I feel very proud that I have been able to get one word out.

'I miss the good old days but,' he says. 'Whole town has changed now, ay?'

Even though he says this with a rising intonation, I know it's really a statement and not a question. I'm relieved that I don't have to answer.

'Everyone is just here for the coin now, ay?' he says.

I nod.

'Not like the good old days when we was kids and everyone knew everyone. Now I come down the street and see no one I know.'

I nod.

'I blame the twelve-hour rosters,' he goes on. 'No one can do nothin' 'cept work. It's bullshit, ay?'

I just keep nodding and smiling. I don't feel the same nostalgia that Bruce clearly feels, but I agree that twelve-hour rotating shifts are not conducive to building community. People are either on four-day or seven-day rosters, which makes it hard to maintain regular commitments to any other community activities.

'And don't get me started on them bloody fly-in, fly-out bastards.'

No chance of that, I think.

'No one cares about the town no more. All they care about is that bloody stinking smoke coming out of the stack,' he says.

'Yeah,' I say. 'It's an environmental nightmare.'

'A what?' Bruce asks.

'Oh … you know, the pollution.'

My voice fades away. Bruce cocks his head and asks, 'Are you a greenie?'

I pause. For a moment I wonder if I should tell him about the traces of lead from the smelter that have been found as far west as Broome. But I don't have to worry as Bruce just barrels on. 'Good on ya,' he says. 'I'd be a greenie too if I didn't have to put food on the table.'

It's impossible not to smile.

'People earn more now, but I reckon it was better when we didn't earn as much and had more community.'

'Me too, Bruce, me too!'

Bruce gives me his wide smile. 'Can't believe I'm talking to ya!' he says. 'I remember when you were on TV.'

'Yep,' I say. 'Nineteen seventy-seven, *A Way with Words*.'

'Debatin' show, wasn't it?'

I nod.

'I liked that show,' says Bruce. 'Your team was the winning one, ay?'

I nod. I am amazed he has remembered this.

'I didn't think you'd ever come back here,' says Bruce.

'I'm looking after Mum,' I tell him.

'Still live in the same house near the park?' he asks.

'Yep,' I say.

'Your mum must be old as now, ay?'

'Ninety-two,' I say.

'Ninety-two! Fuck, that's old, ay!'

I smile and nod.

'Anyway, I gotta go. I got the missus waiting in the car and she'll crack the shits if she knows I'm wasting me time in here yarning on.' Bruce laughs, so I do too. He reaches out his hand and we shake. He's still grinning from ear to ear. 'Good to see ya!' he says.

'You too,' I say.

'True, you haven't changed one bit, not one little bit. I'd recognise you anywhere!' Bruce gives me one last wave and leaves.

The pharmacist hands me the medication and asks, 'How's your mum?'

For the briefest of moments I wonder what to say. Do I tell her that some nights Mum isn't good at all, and Tony and I go to bed wondering if she'll make it through the night, only to be woken by the sound of her humming in the morning?

Or do I tell her that some days I come home from work and find Mum slumped in her chair, and have to sit her up and give her water and sponge her down with a damp cold washer until she becomes lucid again?

Or do I tell her that sometimes Mum loses control of her bowels, and I find traces of faeces on her clothes and bed linen, and have to organise her to have extra showers?

I don't. I say everything is fine and give her a smile. And it's true. Mum is fine; we're all fine. There's nothing more we can say.

I swing out of the car park and head north to the big bridge. I think about Bruce – I still can't place him. I ring my brother Dave.

'What's he look like?' Dave asks.

'He's as tall as he is wide,' I say, and Dave laughs. 'He has a sister called Karen,' I go on. 'Apparently she's still a bitch.'

Dave laughs again. He can't place Bruce or Karen, and he tells me I should check with Mum. 'She'll know for sure.'

I agree.

'How is Mum?' Dave asks.

'She's good. Waiting for me at home to watch *Letters and Numbers*.'

'Youse are doing a good job, you and Tony, a real good job,' Dave says. 'You know that, hey?'

'Yeah,' I say.

'I gotta go. Gotta get a crane hooked up and get it back to Mackay. Talk to ya on the weekend. Love ya.'

'Love ya too,' I say, but I think he's already hung up.

I tear up Madang Street, see Maleka and give her a last-minute swerve. I wouldn't say that I've begun to like Maleka, but my current bonhomie has made me far more compassionate towards her. We have, of late, developed a more convivial relationship. She's stopped barking every time she sees me, and occasionally even comes into our yard for a sit in the shade.

My latest issue with Shawn and Cheyenne are their chooks. They are completely free range, and dig up my seedlings and destroy the small gardens that we have set up under the frangipani trees. Rather than screaming at Maleka, I currently spend a portion of each day chasing the chooks out of our yard with the broom. The young couple who live on the other side of us tell us that they often come home and find the chooks having a dip in their pool.

I pull into the backyard and notice Tony is not home yet. I was hoping he'd get back in time to watch *Letters and Numbers* with us. He's not as much of a fan as I am, but he's alert and fast and it makes the competitive nature of the show all the more enjoyable. It's a fun thing for us to do together.

I look at my watch as I rush up the back ramp. Twenty-seven minutes past five. 'Quick,' I say to Mum, 'stand up so I can move your chair.'

Mum stands and I move her chair so it faces the television. 'I've made a pot of tea,' she tells me.

'Great!' I grab two cups and pour the tea. I turn on the TV and we're right on time. I plonk onto the couch as the opening tune, ticking clock and visuals appear. I take a sip and think, 'This is living!'

Mum and I both play well in the first round. Mum makes a seven-letter word and I solve the numbers game. We both have our strong areas, and we both play with competitive determination. We like doing well. Just before the ad break, the host gives the clue for the first word mix: 'What can housework and airlines both have in common? The clue is COST DIME.'

I mute the TV so we don't have to listen to the ads.

'Cost dime,' says Mum. She writes the words in the air with her finger.

'Housework and airlines,' I say.

'Cos, dos, time, tic, stime, dom,' says Mum.

'Domestic!' I say.

'Good one!' says Mum.

We are on a roll tonight.

'Who would you invite over for a dinner party,' I ask Mum. 'Richard, David or Lily?' They're the hosts of the show.

'Who else would be at the dinner?' Mum asks.

'Tony, you and me. As well as either Richard, David or Lily, you could have two others so there are six at the table.'

'Yes. The table is good for six. I'll use the Noritake,' says Mum.

'Nice,' I say. 'And we can use the linen tablecloth you bought in New York with the six matching serviettes.'

'It'll all need ironing!' says Mum. She sounds almost panicked.

'I'll get started now!' I say, and make to jump up. I turn and look at Mum and we both crack up.

'Who would you invite?' I ask again, once I've stopped laughing.

'All of them,' she says. 'With us and them, we'd have the perfect six at the table.'

'I agree,' I say.

Mum drinks her tea and we sit in silence, waiting for our show to come back on. I think about an Andrew Denton interview Mum and I watched years ago. The guest was a well-known Australian writer. She was funny, intelligent and animated. She had a broad mouth and excellent teeth. Denton didn't need to do much in the way of talking as she chattered liberally and fulsomely. I was quite taken by her. At the end of the show, I said to Mum, 'Wasn't she wonderful?'

Mum just gave a simple nod.

Undeterred, I gushed on. 'I'd love to meet her. Don't you think she'd be fun to have at a dinner party?'

Mum thought about this and then replied, 'I do think that one might find her to be rather socially tiresome.'

Even in my state of excitement I could see just how right Mum was, and just how funny her statement was. What a genteel way to describe someone who takes up all the airtime.

The second part of the show begins and I turn the sound back on. Mum is on fire. She gets another seven-letter word and then a six-letter word.

Tony comes home midway through the show. Mum and I both smile at him but he knows we won't talk until the ad break. He knows the routine so does not take offence. He sits at the kitchen table and reads the newspaper.

I look across at him and can see that he's tired. Tomorrow he has tennis, and on the weekend we're going to Melbourne together for a few days to pack up our house and move our things into storage. It's going to be a huge job, but I also think it'll be the change of scenery that Tony needs.

The credits roll and that's our show for another night.

'What's the plan for dinner?' asks Mum.

'I thought I might heat up the pies we made on the weekend, Diana,' Tony says, 'and have them with mashed potato and steamed green beans.'

'That sounds nice,' Mum says. 'I'll do the potatoes while you water the garden.'

Tony and I go outside. We stand on the back ramp and look at the sunset. The sky is glowing red and pink.

'It's beautiful,' says Tony.

'Yep,' I say. 'You don't get this down in Melbourne, do ya?'

Tony smiles but says nothing.

We spend the next hour watering. I love being outside, and quite like hand-watering but we've got too much grass. We water every second day, the grass grows, and every three weeks we pay someone to come and mow it. The grass looks nice but we only sit on one small part of it. I feel like it's a waste of water, time and money.

'I think I have become an anti-lawnist,' I say to Tony.

'Is that a word?' he asks.

'It should be,' I say.

'Do you think we should concrete everything?'

'Yeah, concrete it or plant it out with edible plants or natives or water-efficient plants, but just get rid of all the wasted grass.'

Tony goes to the shed and comes back with the crowbar. 'Where do you want me to dig the new holes?' he asks.

We walk around the backyard and look at spots where we'll put more plants. Tony starts to dig the holes and I continue to water.

After a while I can smell the pies heating up in the oven and feel hungry. I'm looking forward to dinner. I see the neighbour's chooks scratching around under the trees, and pick them up and put them over the fence. I watch them scurry back to their coop. We still have the crossword to finish from the weekend paper, there's ice cream for dessert, and after dinner I'll play a game of Upwords with Mum.

When we finally get into bed, I tell Tony about my conversation with Bruce. With the excitement of *Letters and Numbers* and watering and Upwords and ice cream, I had forgotten to tell him.

Tony laughs. 'Did you ask Diana if she knew who Bruce was?'

'Nah,' I say.

'Why not?' asks Tony.

'I couldn't be bovvered,' I say.

Tony laughs and turns out the light.

12

TRYING TO ESCAPE

Tony

The sun edges over the western horizon as the small Rex airlines plane eases into the sky and turns its nose northeast, towards Cairns. I'm heading for a job interview. When I applied a couple of weeks earlier, both Beck and I had been open to the possibility. I'd fly back once a month for a long weekend, and Beck would also come to Cairns once a month, which would mean we'd be apart for no longer than two weeks at any one time. Beck likes Cairns, and maybe after Diana died we could live there for a while before returning to Melbourne. The job would be hugely interesting, working on native title business up and down the Cape.

The western sky has gone from yellow to red, and the shades of blue in the sky above are graded from a thin washed-out blue, through a rich navy, to a star-inflected purplish black. I try to imagine doing this flight on a monthly basis – FIFO in reverse, heading away from the mining town for work, not to it. There's a romantic appeal. I conjure up a sun-filled bungalow in Cairns, set amid a tropical garden and raised off the ground to capture the breeze from the

Coral Sea. I would put myself on small planes darting up and down the Cape, meeting with the traditional owners and drawing maps in the dirt. I allow the fantasy to meander as we fly through the darkening sky, accompanied by the steady hum of the engines.

We land, and as I wander through the almost empty terminal towards the taxi rank, I realise with absolute clarity that the plan will never work. I don't want this lonely life. The feeling is compounded over the next couple of hours as I check into my hotel and walk the streets looking for food. It's Monday night and the streets are even emptier than the airport. Eventually I find a Thai place that's open, and order pad thai with fresh chillies to take back to my room. Rebecca, Diana and our cosy little Madang Street world seem so far away.

The next morning, despite my building misgivings, I bring my A game to the interview, which lasts nearly two hours. I know the job will be mine by the time I leave. When the boss, Peter, rings and offers me the job a couple of days later, I'm caught in a bind. The job appeals to me greatly. I really connected with Peter and the two traditional owners who interviewed me. I know the job will be interesting, and I want out of my current job. I play for time and tell Peter I'll give him an answer after the weekend. I'm not sure what I'm hoping for, but perhaps something will happen in the intervening days that will somehow make taking the job the only sensible option. Perhaps we can make the maths work, and the frequency of my trips back to Mount Isa and Beck's trips to Cairns will make the time apart less consequential. Perhaps Beck will decide that she and her mum will follow, and we'll all live in Cairns happily until Diana dies. Perhaps I'll conclude that it's truly impossible for me to continue where I am and that I have no other option.

But I know none of these is likely. I also know that I could push and Beck would give her endorsement and try to make it work.

But that feels like me getting my own way, a repeat of previous big decisions where my needs edged out Beck's.

And when it comes down to it, I like our Mount Isa world. I don't want to dismantle what we've got and what we've committed to. Furthermore, I don't want to triangulate our centres of gravity by adding Cairns to Melbourne and Mount Isa. I'm sure I can manage the tensions with head office.

On Monday evening after work I call Peter. 'I can't take the job,' I tell him. 'I'm disappointed.'

'I am too,' he replies.

'It just won't work with the family. But thank you.'

'I understand. We'll find someone else. Good luck,' he tells me.

'You too.' I hang up.

I take myself outside to water the garden. The sun is setting and the hills are aglow. Relief courses through me.

I put my head down at work and get on with it. Despite the fence topped with barbed wire that runs around the office, Bernice and I try to make the place as welcoming as possible to the various native title holders in the district. The local mob are the Kalkadoon, but in the area surrounding are the Pitta Pitta, Mitakoodi, Yulina, Bularnu, Waluwarra and Wangkangujuru, just to name a few. And many of them have made their homes in Mount Isa and are actively involved in managing their native title interests.

From time to time some will drop in on the pretext of getting the details of a forthcoming meeting or signing a form of some sort, but I know they really just want a chat. I often make a cup of tea and we sit out under the carport in the heat so they can smoke. I love listening to their stories of growing up on the stations. Many of the older generation were born on one of the stations in the area, such as Roxborough, Glenormiston and Headingly. Many of them were kids when they moved to Dajarra, the biggest town in the area at the time, and the focal point for the stock routes that ran from the west. Cattle were driven there and then put on trains bound for the east coast. The families followed the cattle and work, and sent their kids to school in town. Eventually, as trucks took over from trains, and more mines opened up, Mount Isa became the bigger town, and over time many families moved here. This and the granting of equal pay to Aboriginal stockmen in 1968 led to an exodus from the bush. The pastoralists were only prepared to employ white people, and closed down the Aboriginal camps. The dispossession which had commenced a hundred years earlier was now complete.

Today Lance has called in. He does so a lot, and this time I'm busy preparing documents for a meeting and so I give him short shrift. 'I gotta get this document finished, Lance. What can I do for you?'

'All I need's the phone.'

'No worries,' I tell him.

He rings the works supervisor for the Boulia Shire Council and lines up a walk. This involves surveying an area where the council plans to do some work – widen a road, put in a drain, extract gravel – to ensure that no cultural heritage will be damaged.

Lance hangs up and gives me a nod. 'Gotta do a walk at Headingly. Taking me nephew along.' He leaves happy, knowing that in a couple of days he'll be back out on country and getting paid for it.

Georgina and Lucille and my eldest sister, Anne, come to town to visit, and also to go camping at Boodjamulla (Lawn Hill) National

Park. Diana's little house bulges. I can see that Diana is shy around Anne, and retreats into her green chair and into herself. I know this upsets Beck and puts her on edge. She wants everyone to see the fun, smart and welcoming side of Diana, not this closed-off one. But Anne is very kind and capable socially, and is not easily deterred. Soon she has Diana back at the kitchen table, playing Upwords.

It's fantastic to have the girls here – it's the first occasion since we've been living here. This time with them is very important for us, but I realise when they arrive that it's also very important for them. It's easy for me to think that our move up here is having no impact on them. Beck and I both left home at seventeen. Our girls are in their early twenties, so what's the big deal? I don't think I'm prepared to admit that kids leaving home at the time of their choosing and circling back to the family home, which is static and known, is very different to our situation, where the parents have left the kids behind, thereby turning the natural order on its head.

With the nieces lined up to call in on Diana daily, and a solemn promise from Diana to wear her alarm, we load up the big four-wheel drive and take off for Lawn Hill. We travel west on the Barkly Highway for an hour, then turn north towards the Gregory River. An hour later we cross a cattle grid and I notice a sign: Undilla Station. I turn to Beck. 'Remember that poster when we first came to town about the kid who went missing?' Beck nods. 'This is the place where he was last seen.' Anne, Georgina and Luci in the back seat prick up their ears and I tell them the story, as much as I know it.

A little over two years ago, Kyle Coleman, seventeen, and James Coleman, twenty-one – not related but friends and work colleagues – came out here camping, shooting and drinking. Only James made it back. No one has seen Kyle since, nor have any traces of his remains been discovered.

The two had loaded up James's ute with grog and guns and headed for an overnight camping trip along the Gregory River, three hundred kilometres away. Due to heavy rain they couldn't get through to the river, and turned instead into Undilla Station. The manager gave them permission to camp but advised they wouldn't get past the first creek crossing. The manager was the last person – other than James – to see Kyle alive. From this point on, the story gets very muddy, much like the rain-soaked dirt tracks the young men went down.

James returned alone to Mount Isa that night or early the next morning. He told the police they had hung around the station for a while, drinking and shooting cans with a .303 rifle, before returning to Mount Isa. In his statement, James said they drank the rest of the alcohol at his house, and then he went inside to go to the toilet and when he came out Kyle was gone. Four days later, James hanged himself in the back shed of his parents' house.

I was able to tell the story in detail as the coroner's findings had only just been released, and I had read the report with morbid fascination. The coroner found that Kyle was shot by James on Undilla Station, and that James burnt Kyle's belongings, including his swag and his backpack, which contained his watch and his timesheet book. She found that James Coleman was deliberately untruthful when he said that he and Kyle had returned to Mount Isa together. Despite this, she found that they had been good friends when they left to go camping, and there was no evidence of animosity or a falling-out between them, or that James had any motive to harm Kyle. The coroner concluded that there was no evidence to infer the death was anything other than accidental.

As we drive along, I wonder what had happened out here. Was it merely a drunken accident or did they have a fight? Was James jealous of Kyle's friendship with his girlfriend? Was there an unrequited attraction of one to the other? Did they argue about the car Kyle was buying from James, or something to do with work? I think of Kyle's parents, who'll never know what happened to their son, and of James's parents, who not only have the sadness of their son's death but also the guilt and shame of knowing he lied and died by his own hand, taking all the answers with him. I look out the window and imagine Kyle's bones lying somewhere out here. Scattered by animals among the low hills, rocks and dry creek beds, or perhaps shoved down an old mine shaft.

We bounce along the dirt road, lost in our thoughts.

Back in Mount Isa, the camping trip and the family visit recede from my mind. I'm offered an interview for a senior native title job in the Torres Strait. I decline the interview for all the reasons I turned down the Cape York job, but not without first indulging a fantasy of laid-back island living, eating fresh seafood and snorkelling in crystal-clear waters.

I also interview for an Indigenous family violence legal job in Mount Isa. I like the people who interview me, and I'm attracted to the idea of travelling the circuit, flying in and out of remote communities, appearing in local courts. But at the end of the interview we discuss money, and the salary doesn't come close to what I'm currently on so I withdraw my application. I put my head down and get on with my job.

I'm home for lunch with Diana. Beck is at work. Diana toys with her lunch and stands to make her way back to the recliner. She is suddenly immobilised, the colour drains from her face and her eyes roll back. I move forwards but I'm too late, and Diana crumples to the floor.

I immediately remember the time this happened with Beck alone, when Diana couldn't get back to her feet. Then Beck had been forced to call an ambulance. Diana tries to get up. I tell her to wait and bring a chair close by. Together, with her climbing on the chair and me lifting, she manages to get on her feet and I escort her to the recliner. I make her a cup of tea.

'Do you think you need to go to the hospital?' I ask.

Diana shakes her head. 'No, I'll be fine.'

I text Bernice and I tell her what's happened, and that I'll spend the rest of the day working from home. She tells me she's got it covered and to let me know if I need anything.

I also text Beck. First I describe what happened, then:

No need to come home. She's fine.

Beck replies:
You sure?

Me:
Yep.

Beck:
She's sort of shutting down, isn't she?

Me:
Yep.

Beck:
Not a bad way to go, I suppose. Peaceful.

Me:
Yep.

Beck:
Is that all you've got to say?

Me:
Yep.

Beck:
You almost seem pleased!

Me:
Yep.

Beck:
Ha. See you when I get home.

Me:
Yep!

13

FROM FAR AWAY

Rebecca

I'm walking past my desk at Headspace when I notice my phone flashing. It's on silent so there is no sound. I can see it's Lucille calling via Facebook. I've never had a phone call via Facebook before, and am momentarily surprised. At the same time, I register that Lucille, who is studying in the Netherlands, rarely calls unless we've arranged a time. Something must be wrong.

'Lu?'

I hear a gulped inward breath, and know that it's the sound of a sob being sucked back. She finds air and pushes out one word: 'Mum—' And then her voice gives way to tears and static, but with that one word I know that her relationship is over.

I walk past my desk and out into the corridor. I need to find somewhere private to talk. I can hear Lucille crying and at the same time trying to catch her breath and speak.

'Don't speak,' I say. 'Just breathe.'

I quickly scan the doors of the counselling rooms and see they are all occupied. I open the door to the medical examination room:

it's empty. I go inside and shut the door. I look for a chair but there isn't one. I contemplate climbing up on the medical examination table but that feels like a step too far, even for me.

I lean against the wall and keep talking to Lu. 'In, two, three, hold, two, three, four, out, two, three, four, five …'

She knows what to do. We have done this before.

As Lucille works on her breathing, I tell her softly, 'This is normal; what you are feeling is normal; you've done nothing wrong. Don't try to speak, just follow your breathing; soon we will talk.' I sense that she is nodding.

Slowly her breathing calms. As it does, her sobs turn to gentle tears. I look at the world clock on my phone and realise it is 8 am in the Netherlands. She doesn't have good wi-fi in her apartment so I wonder where she is.

I wait until her tears ease, and then ask, 'Where are you?'

'At the uni campus.' She has ridden her bike from her apartment, and has found a corner in a building where she can access the free wi-fi. 'I just got out of bed and came here,' she says.

'In your trackie dacks?' I ask.

She cries again, and in between the sobs I hear her laugh as she describes how she looks. This is a good sign.

'Yeah,' she says, 'I look terrible. I haven't washed my face or combed my hair.'

She tells me that the text was waiting for her when she woke up. It confirmed the end of their relationship. She knew it was coming; she had wondered who would do it first. Though she's in love, she knows it's not a good relationship and understands that the only real solution is for it to end. But untangling and letting go is never easy. Someone had to do it and now it is done.

It's been a relationship that enjoyed a blissful period, but over many months spiralled into a place of confusion, pain and dislike for them both. It's been on again and off again, and all of us have been through the highs and lows with Lu. They have both behaved, at times, poorly, but also respectfully. Though I don't say it, I'm relieved it's over.

I have nothing against her beau. In fact, my feelings are quite the opposite – I am very fond of him, and Tony and I have both talked about how we will miss him, though we both knew it had to and would end. He is a beautiful young man but I could sense the writing was on the wall when we were all together in Japan; his moodiness and fragility and her eagerness to please and vulnerability created a fundamental inequality that not even love could save.

Standing in the medical exam room, I look at the rows of boxes of latex gloves, speculums, condoms and lube. I contemplate telling Lucille where I am and what I'm surrounded by, as I know it will amuse her, but decide against it. I can hear her trying to gulp back the tears so that she can talk.

'I want to come home!' she sobs.

I tell her not to make any decisions right now; that she does not need to understand everything. 'Just allow the tears to come.' I tell her that she took a risk, a risk with love, and that is something to be proud of. Some people go through life never feeling brave enough to take that risk.

I tell her no one is to blame and no one is innocent, and that she will get over this. She should take as long as she needs, and know that I am here for her.

The door to the room opens. I jerk my head up and see one of my colleagues standing there. 'I thought you'd gone home,' she says.

I put my hand over the phone and quickly tell her what I'm doing. She nods knowingly, smiles and tells me that everyone's leaving, and asks if I can lock up the building when I'm finished. She asks me if I'm okay. I smile and nod, and for the millionth time think how lucky I am to have this job and these people.

I go back to the phone. We talk about what Lu is going to do today. She has plans, and I feel relieved that she's busy. I encourage her to steer clear of drinking too much and using social media. This elicits a wry laugh.

She asks me what I'm going to do with my day, and I tell her I'm about to go home from work. She laughs again and tells me she had no idea what time it was when she rang, but that she just had to.

'I know!' I laugh.

We talk pleasantries and her breathing steadies even more. I make a point of being upbeat, of keeping my energy up, of not saying anything that could trigger a fresh bout of tears.

'How's Grandma?' she asks.

I don't have the heart to tell her about the recent fainting episode in Woolworths, or the sprained ankle, or that she needs to get a wheelie walker and that she is very resistant, or how she seems now to have more bad days than good. I don't want to give her any more reason to think about coming home.

'She's good,' I say.

'That's good,' Lu says.

She says she needs go. I say yes. She says, 'I love you,' and is gone.

I punch the numbers into the alarm code at Headspace, pull the door shut behind me and jiggle the handle to make sure it's locked. As I step outside I'm hit by a blast of hot air. I look up and squint. The sun stills seems far too high in the sky for this hour of the day.

I realise that I haven't left the building all afternoon, and had completely forgotten how bloody hot it is out here. I long to step out of my work building or the house and be hit by a cool change, but that won't happen until about April next year.

I stand outside and think about what I'll do now. I should just get in the car and go home but I feel agitated and I don't want to. Not even the lure of *Letters and Numbers* excites me.

I rarely say this, but today I want to be in Melbourne.

I want to be on my bike and riding home through the Edinburgh Gardens. I want to feel the cool air on my face as I ride through the park and see people hanging out with their dogs, skateboards and beers.

I want to meet a friend on Lygon Street, have a cheap pasta meal and then go and see a play at La Mama.

I want to go home to my own house, run a bath, pour a glass of wine, drink it in the bath and not think about anything or anyone.

I want to call a friend and talk about love and life and children and heartache and the best solutions for maintaining one's dignity when the chips are down.

I want to cook dahl, brown rice and steamed greens, and eat it in bed while I read a book or watch something on my computer.

I want to be anywhere but here.

I stand on the footpath and think. I could go home and get my togs and go to the pool, but I know myself well enough to realise that once I get home I won't leave again.

I could drive out to the lake and go for a walk, but I would feel mean doing that without Mum or Tony. I could go and visit my nieces or ring my friend Majella and see if she wants to come and have a drink. But I'm too agitated, and a drink is the last thing I need.

I walk up the street and go to the newsagent. This is the only shop here that's open after 5.30 pm. I know the fella who owns it – we went to school together. I feel comfortable here. I pick up a bag of lollies and tell myself they're for Mum, but I know I will eat them all myself, on the sly, in the car. I select a few postcards that I'll probably never send. I pick up a magazine about gardening and decide to get it too.

I pay for my things and walk to my car. I get in, start driving and before I even realise it I'm heading up the Barkly Highway towards home. This reminds me of Dad. As kids, we used to say that his Kingswood could travel on autopilot. He could be blind drunk but still the car would make it home safely. I hated that he drove when he was drunk and used to pray that the police would pull him over, but it never happened.

Sometimes, when he couldn't face Mum or us kids, he would go to his sister's house in the next street. We would ride past on our bikes and see his car parked out the front, but we knew not to go in. Aunty Eileen was pretty straight up and down and never seemed too perturbed by him; she would let him sleep it off at her place before sending him home.

Sometimes he would be so drunk that he would open the car door, fall out and then crawl up the back steps.

I remember one very hot Saturday afternoon. We heard the Kingswood come around the corner. We all went to the kitchen widow and watched Dad manoeuvre the car through the gate. It's quite narrow, and how Dad managed was a pretty good indicator of how drunk he was.

He drove very slowly; this was not good. Mum said nothing but we all felt the energy change.

The car stalled about fifteen metres from the house. We watched as the driver's door opened and Dad fell out, landing on the dirt driveway. We all looked at each other, but said nothing. Eventually, we moved away from the window and more or less forgot that Dad was down there. He was never home on a Saturday afternoon so it was all much of a muchness.

A couple of hours later Mum said to Paul, 'It's very hot out there – go and check on your father.'

I didn't go outside with Paul, but watched from the back door. I wanted to help but knew that Mum would be annoyed if I did. Although I was a child, I knew what was happening: this was political. Mum was furious with Dad and wanted to punish him. She knew she needed to look after him but she also wanted him to suffer.

Paul went downstairs, looked at Dad and then went under the house. He came back with two star pickets, a tarp and some rope, and made a beautiful awning over the car door to cover Dad. Now he was in full shade.

Paul, too, understood the politics of the situation. If he brought Dad into the house he would probably wake up and start drinking again. This would make Mum angry. But he knew that he needed to protect Dad as much as he could. I assume Paul gave Dad some water from the hose, too.

At about six o'clock Dad woke and slowly came upstairs. He had a shower, ate something and then went to bed. Paul packed up the temporary shelter and parked the car under the house. Nobody said anything further about it.

I see Maleka sitting in her regular spot in the middle of the road, and blast the horn at her. As usual she doesn't move, and I have to swerve around her.

I pull slowly into the driveway and see Tony in the backyard doing the hand-watering. I tell him what has happened. We both stand without speaking, and watch him fill up the oasis that we have made around the fruit trees.

I go inside and am surprised to see Mum in the kitchen. I ask her what she's doing and she says brightly, 'I'm peeling tatties, Kathleen!'

I can't help but laugh. She offers to make me a cup of tea. She's in fine fettle, and with that my malaise shifts.

I put the tatties on the stove and we take our tea out to the verandah.

'How was your rehab class?' I ask.

'Awesome!' Mum says.

I laugh. 'Did you say that to the staff at the hospital?'

'I did,' she says.

'And what did they say?' I ask.

'They laughed!' says Mum.

I think of the expression 'the apple doesn't fall far from the tree'. Mum and I both love making people laugh. It's not so much that we want other people to think we're funny; it's the joy we get from seeing other people laugh.

'What else did you do, besides making people laugh?' I ask.

'I moved things from one box to another, stood up and sat down, lay on the bed and showed them that I could sit up unaided, and walked through a sort of stepping maze.'

'Sound great,' I say.

'It all sounds a bit silly, but when I'm there and doing the exercises it all makes complete sense,' she says.

I'm surprised at how much Mum is enjoying these rehab classes. It's one of the two good things that have come out of the sprained ankle. The other is the wheelie walker.

'Are you still going to do the trip out with the physiotherapist so that you can practise with a wheelie walker?' I ask her.

'Yes, she's going to come around as soon as the wheelie walker arrives.'

I hope that's soon. Legacy has kindly offered to pay for the walker. Mum's friend Beryl is helping us get it organised. The process for organising any sort of aid for elderly people seems to take an inordinate amount of time. I often think about people who don't have family or friends to help them navigate the system. How do they manage?

We've discussed the wheelie walker with Mum's GP, the practice nurse at the GP clinic and the staff at community health, and have spent a ridiculous amount of time navigating the My Aged Care website. Everyone seems to have a different sense of what we need to do. Fingers crossed that we've finally worked out how to proceed, and that the wheelie walker will be here soon.

'That's generous of her,' I say about the physiotherapist.

'We're going to visit the places I go to regularly,' Mum says.

'Good,' I say. 'Did she ask you what those places were?'

Mum nods.

'I told her Woolworths, church and the Irish Club.'

'The Irish Club! Why did you suggest there?' I ask. 'You don't go there very often.'

'I go there for Legacy lunches, and it's so dark inside,' she says. 'I thought it would be a good place to practise.'

'She might think you have a thing for the pokies, Mum.'

'She might,' Mum agrees.

'Or that you're an old soak!'

Mum laughs.

'Lucille rang while I was at work,' I tell her.

'Is she okay?' Mum asks.

'She's broken up for good with Max,' I say, and I tell her about the phone call.

She listens, and then asks, 'Do you feel a long way from her?'

I hesitate before answering. If I say yes, it might create a situation where Mum feels bad about the fact that I'm here with her and not somewhere else with my daughter; if I say no, it denies the fact that I'm here and would be dishonest.

'Yes, I do,' I say. 'But it makes no difference whether I'm in Mount Isa or Melbourne. Lucille is on the other side of the world, and I hate it that she's sad.'

This is why I feel flat and out of sorts. It has nothing to do with being in Mount Isa or not being in Melbourne or with having to look after Mum. My baby is in pain.

Mum tells me she understands this feeling. She starts to talk about the various distraught phone calls I made over the years. I groan and roll my eyes, and we laugh about how dramatic I was about everything.

'Ha,' I say, 'those phones calls were always a lifesaver. Hearing your voice was all I usually needed.'

She laughs. 'I'm glad they made you feel better, because they always made me feel worse!'

She's told me this before, and it always reminds me how selfish children can be, and how much we take for granted with our parents.

I tell Mum that Lucille doesn't need me to solve her problems or run to her rescue, she just needs me to listen. 'It's what you always provided for me, and now it's my turn,' I say.

Mum nods, and we sit without speaking. I remember the lollies in my bag and go inside and get them. We sit in comfortable silence, eating our lollies and watching Tony water the front yard. I wonder if this might be the time for me to ask a few big questions.

How did Mum feel when Michael was 'on the run' for all those years?

How did she feel when my nephew was accidentally killed?

How did she feel when Michael himself died?

How did she feel when Dad would sink into a period of rage and despair?

How did she feel when she withdrew from society and holed up at home with her pain and shame?

How does she feel about the fact that her sister hasn't spoken to her for the last thirty-seven years?

In the past, I have pushed and prodded Mum to talk about her feelings. I place a great deal of value on talking about how you feel. Mum believes that what is done is done.

The year before I moved back to Mount Isa, I tried to push her into telling me what happened with her sister. Foolishly, I decided to do this over the phone. The conversation didn't go well. Mum retreated into irritated denial and then silence. I could tell I had upset her, and after a stilted conversation she hung up.

The next day I rang her back to apologise. She told me that she had been very upset; so upset, in fact, that she had tripped over a power cord and hit her face on the top of the oil heater, and now had a black eye and a cut on her face. I felt awful about this. Reluctantly, I agreed to not discuss it anymore.

Over the last eighteen or so months I've been waiting for this moment, waiting for the floodgates to open, waiting to be the dutiful daughter who is there for her mother when the day of reckoning comes.

'We used to sit out here when you were small,' Mum says.

'I remember,' I say.

Mum seems surprised to hear this. 'What do you remember?'

'Michael doing handstands and cartwheels; Dad walking on his hands; us other kids doing wheelbarrow races; the dog, probably Flash, tearing around and barking.'

Mum smiles. 'You remember all that?'

'Yes.'

Mum smiles.

'Dad would put on the sprinkler, and we'd run through and pretend it was a swimming pool,' I say.

'I'm glad you have some good memories,' she says.

'I have lots of those.'

I wait for Mum to speak.

She takes another lolly. 'These are nice, fresh.'

'Yes,' I say.

We sit without speaking, and I'm struck by how calm Mum is. In this moment she seems happy and content. I think about what I said to Lu about remaining in the present, about not rehashing the past or worrying about the future, and I realise that this is Mum. After all those years of turmoil, incredibly she now seems to have the capacity to just be in the moment.

There is no need to go back over all these things. Yes, it would be good to know how Mum felt and what happened – but good for her or for me? Maybe she's right; maybe some things are best just left in the past.

14

THE ELEPHANT IN THE ROOM

Tony

It's eight-thirty in the morning and I'm thinking of death. Last week I flew to Brisbane to attend Brad's funeral; the melanoma finally got the better of him. I'd said my final farewell to Brad by text. Twice, in fact. The first time was in April, when he took a serious turn for the worse. 'Thanks, mate. I'm on the way out, I reckon,' he replied. He lived for another four months. The second time around, days before he died, I texted him: 'You're in my thoughts, good friend. I've had great adventures with you, Brad. I'm richer for them all. You're off on another now, on your own. Go well. Love, Tony.' He didn't reply.

Now I'm outside Diana's door. Beck's away and I need to go to work, but Diana hasn't emerged from her room. Normally she'd have been up for hours by now. I try to recall if I heard her up and about throughout the night. Some nights she and I both lie awake, listening to the dogs barking, the desert wind whistling through the louvres and the trains shunting in the railyards on the other side of the highway. I would hear her shuffling to the toilet at some stage through the night, and no doubt she would hear me pissing loudly into the bowl on the other side of the wall from her bed, until I remembered to direct the flow to the side of the toilet.

I'm not entirely sure what to do. I don't want to disturb her if she's had a bad night's sleep and has only just now drifted off, but she could be dead.

Tentatively, I knock on the door. 'Diana? I'm off to work. Are you okay?'

'Yes, I'm fine.' Her reply is clipped.

Disappointment rushes through me, not relief, and this both surprises and embarrasses me. My wish for a swift and peaceful death must be stronger than I realise. How easy it would be for Diana, and how easy it would make life for us. No more continual contemplation of our future. No more juggling two places. No more bloody Mount Isa. But to wish someone dead seems beyond the pale, despite whatever rational justifications one can summon up.

Diana sleeps in for the next three mornings. Each day I knock on the door before leaving the house and get the same response: 'I'm fine.'

I tell Beck over the phone, and we wonder if this is the beginning of the end. A slow and steady decline, until finally she stops breathing in her chair or doesn't wake up from her sleep. Beck doesn't seem particularly disturbed or saddened by this prospect; in fact, I sense that she too would feel some relief if it happened this way, and soon. She knows her mother's death is inevitable, and that there's a whole range of slow and difficult alternatives that Diana could face. That we all could face.

By the time Beck returns a couple of days later, Diana is past the worst and is back to her relatively perky self. She flogs both of us at Upwords after dinner and spends the next day making a fruitcake.

In counterpoint to the possibility that Diana is close to death, and that our time in Mount Isa might come to an end soon, we are becoming more and more immersed in the town. We're regulars with the community choir, performing at various events around town. Mainly through Beck, we've formed a small circle of friends. We've been invited to dinner twice now, and have even hosted a small dinner party ourselves. We both play tennis regularly, and I recently became secretary of the local tennis club. Like many clubs in town, it has suffered from the mine's switch to a seven-day twelve-hour roster, which means that every second week employees can't reliably attend events. When I put my hand up to join the committee, I didn't have to compete against a slew of candidates.

Despite our expanding social options, our life is still simpler than it was in Melbourne, and both Beck and I find that we have plenty of time to write, garden and spend time with Diana.

Work has hit a sweet spot. I go on a field trip with my anthropologist colleague James to the coast to talk to the descendants of people rounded up like cattle from the west a hundred years earlier and trucked to either Yarrabah, on the end of a rugged promontory south of Cairns, or Palm Island, fifty-three kilometres northeast of Townsville.

On Palm Island we are invited into Eddie Firebrace's house. I am struck by its neatness. On one side of the kitchen sink a slotted spoon, ladle, egg flip and potato masher hang on the wall. On the other side, sugar, coffee, Milo, tea and powdered milk containers sit in a row on the bench. Two sheets are folded with precision on the bed next to the table; I am itching to ask why the bed is in the kitchen. A handful of photos adorn the otherwise bare walls of the lounge room. An ex-drinker, I think to myself. Eddie is someone who's working hard to maintain control.

I am there with James to talk to Eddie about his grandmother Topsy. Through painstaking archival research, James has discovered that she was one of those 'old people' who were rounded up and brought east. Until now, Eddie didn't know where his grandmother came from. All he knew was that it was from the west somewhere. His family used to live in an area of the community set aside for the 'sundowners' – those people who came from the direction where the sun went down.

A lot of Aboriginal reserves and missions were set up like that, with people from the same group living in enclaves. It was often within these enclaves that laws and customs were maintained, despite the distance, and so they've become vital sources of evidence to support native title claims over country far away. Even if people weren't living on country, they were still connected to it through the practice of their culture, rooted in the country from which they were forcibly removed. Eddie is pleased to finally know, but still I sense his loss at not knowing much about his grandmother and the place she came from.

Over the course of eight days, James and I visit descendants of the sundowners scattered throughout north Queensland, to share what we've found out about their ancestors and learn from them what they know, so that we can form as clear a picture as possible of their native title group. Like other parts of Australia, their country is hotly disputed and has had many failed native title claims. Some of the claimants are descended from ancestors who escaped deportation to the east. They still live on country and some stridently resist the idea that people whose families have not lived on country for a hundred years have a right to be part of the native title group. To me, this feels like dispossession yet again.

A couple of weeks later I have another trip away, this time to central Queensland, to work on another native title claim. They are a capable and compassionate group, and we have a productive couple of days visiting sites and meeting with shire council members and local pastoralists. They have a huge task ahead of them. Long-term dispossession means that proving continuous connection to country – a key requirement in a native title suit – will be difficult.

One pastoralist is particularly sceptical of their claim to native title. 'I've been in the district sixty years and haven't seen a blackfella on my property the whole time,' the pastoralist challenges us as we sit around the boardroom in the council chambers.

'That's because you built a fence around the property,' a claimant replies softly.

Another adds, 'My great-grandfather was taken from here against his will. He tried to come back plenty of times. But always he was picked up by the police and brought back to the mission in chains.'

The pastoralist responds by telling them he grew up on a property in the gulf that had stone outhouses with rifle slits in the walls for shooting blacks if they attacked. I don't really know why he's telling this story. Is he seeking some empathy for his views? *You see, this is where I have come from; I'm not as bad as that.* I can't help but read it as a threat. The others remain respectfully assertive, despite the deep anger that I can tell is bubbling below the surface.

There are plans afoot to build a gas pipeline from Tennant Creek to Mount Isa that will connect the offshore gas fields in the Timor Sea with the east coast markets. It's a big resource infrastructure project that requires land access agreements with over twenty native title groups along its route. Usually negotiations for such agreements take six months or more. One of the groups was initially overlooked until now, and there are only two months left before the deadline for all agreements to be reached. I've been asked to step in and lead the negotiations on behalf of the native title group. I've never negotiated such an agreement before, and although it feels daunting I'm buoyed by the challenge, and by the confidence placed in me.

But there's still the ticking clock of my job back in Melbourne.

I need to return by April next year or resign. This has been in the back of my mind the whole time we've been here, but its reality is impending. To be honest, I'm not as sanguine about it as I like to think. I'll definitely resign if Diana is still alive but I'm anxious about it. What the fuck will I do in Melbourne when we eventually do go back? I'll be in my late fifties, or perhaps sixties. Who will give me a job? Native title law is a limited field, especially in Melbourne.

I consider and reject the idea of private legal practice. I don't have the networks, skills or chutzpah to do that. I could work as a consultant. But it seems to me there are already too many consultants out there scrabbling for work. I'm not Aboriginal, and more and more work in Indigenous affairs is, quite rightly, being done by Indigenous people. And increasingly there are highly competent and qualified Aboriginal and Torres Strait Islander people in the market, available for the work I would be competing for.

'I get it,' I say to Beck from the lounge room. She's at the kitchen table flicking through a magazine and I'm lying on the couch reading. It's late Sunday afternoon and Diana's resting in her room. We have the house wide open and a gentle breeze is circulating.

'Get what?' Beck looks up.

'What you're doing to this place. Simplifying it. Decluttering it.'

'Returning it to its 1950s aesthetic,' Beck adds.

'It looks good. For a small house it sure feels spacious. It has good bones,' I say, and go back to reading my book.

A couple of minutes later, Beck says, 'I can imagine living here after Mum dies.'

I think on it. 'Me too. We could do what everyone else does here – make money and then retire east or south in fifteen years.

It would solve the work problem and make life very easy.'

'The girls would be horrified,' Beck says.

'We can't plan our life around them,' I say. 'They might not stay in Melbourne forever,' I add a few moments later.

'True. But one thing I know for sure is they will never live here,' says Beck with a hint of resignation in her voice.

She has a point.

I continue to read and daydream on the couch. I imagine the other things we would do to the house – open out the dining room onto a deck, renovate the bathroom, plant more and more natives – but at what cost to our family and lives down south?

Again, I find myself awake in the middle of the night, listening to the growl of the mine, the barking of the dogs and the rattling of the wind, worrying about our future and trying to remind myself to trust in life and believe that it'll all work out.

'How did you sleep?' Diana asks when she comes into the kitchen and puts the kettle on.

'Same same,' I reply.

I don't let on that it's worry more than the nocturnal sounds that kept me awake. I have no doubt Diana is aware of the looming deadline; perhaps she's kept awake by worries that in a few months' time we'll pack up and move back to Melbourne despite our promise to stay. Perhaps she's willing herself to die, knowing that the alternatives are too grim to think about. But neither of us acknowledge the elephant in the room.

'The dogs were particularly bad last night,' I add.

'When are they not?' Diana replies.

I get home from work and Diana's inside watching *Letters and Numbers*. I feel the need to be outside, and decide to give the garden a water. I'm halfway through the backyard when Beck pulls into the driveway. She looks flat.

'You okay?' I ask.

'Luci and Max are over. She called me from Utrecht.'

'Shit. How is she?'

'Sad. She couldn't talk at first, she was crying that much.'

'How are you?'

'Yeah, okay, I suppose. I'll fill you in later. I'll go check on Mum.'

Feeling glum, I move around to the front yard. We haven't done much planting on this side of the house; mainly we've tried to bring the hedge back to life, keep the lawn vaguely green and grow pots under the frangipanis. It's very exposed, and the early onset of summer has already given it a caning.

I watch two kites circling in the early evening thermals and listen for the call of the koel that's made a temporary home in the Moreton Bay fig in the park across the road. It's still morning in Utrecht. I think of Luci with her broken heart facing the long day ahead alone.

Beck and Diana come out onto the verandah with cups of tea in hand. Beck throws me a lolly. 'Gotta look after the help,' she quips to Diana.

'Yeah, that's right,' Diana joins in. 'Don't want the help complaining.'

I threaten them with the hose.

After dinner Beck and I go for a walk. We have a set route. Down the length of the park towards town. At the end we turn right and walk to the service road that runs adjacent to the Barkly Highway. We always marvel at the house on the corner with the big, jungly garden, especially the pawpaw trees dripping with plump fruit. Six months ago we planted two pawpaws next to the ramp. They grew quickly and lushly at first and started to fruit, and then suddenly they withered and died. Beck thinks it's our mongrel clay soil, which doesn't drain properly. Although they like a lot of water, pawpaws don't appear to like wet feet.

From the garden house we walk the length of the service road to the First n' Last Store, and then right again along Milne Bay Road to the start of the park. From there it's a few hundred metres back home. This route is relatively free of snarling dogs lunging at fences, and consequently it's Beck's favourite.

'I wonder if one of us should try to get to Utrecht soon,' Beck says as we walk. 'I think Lu will get really homesick and shut down from the experience. She's already saying she wants to come home early.'

I'm amazed at Beck's ability to tap into the emotional world of the girls so acutely. Her empathy and clear thinking has helped both of them navigate the fraught waters of relationships and growing up. I'm concerned, though, that Beck will overly worry about Luci and internalise her pain. I'm tempted to downplay it. Tell Beck that Luci will get over it quickly, and not to worry. On the other hand, a trip to Europe at Christmas doesn't sound too bad. In my mind I'm almost there.

At the side gate we stop and look at the clear sky. The air has a silky texture to it. 'Luci will be okay,' Beck says. 'She's strong and smart. She just feels things so deeply.'

'No one needs to rescue her?'

'Nah. But give her a call in the next day or two.'

'I will.'

Neither of us need to do a mercy dash to Utrecht, but I know when Diana dies our place is back in Melbourne, close to the girls and their lives, at least until they're ready to leave on their own terms.

15

THE END

Rebecca

Leonard Cohen has died, and Mum has spent the week listening to every program about him on the ABC. She asks me when I first heard his music.

I start to tell her about the Canadian I hung out with in Pokhara, in Nepal, in early 1988, but Mum butts in. 'Is he the one who helped you out when you were sick in Kathmandu?'

'Yep,' I say.

'Are you still in touch?'

'Nope.'

'That's a shame. I wonder what happened to him.'

I don't answer. She knows I'm no longer in contact with the Canadian – she's asked me this before. These are standard questions from Mum. She asks me if I'm still in touch with every person I have ever known or spoken about. I find it infuriating. 'Do you want to hear my story in Pokhara?'

She nods.

'It was early evening, and we were walking along a dusty

223

street looking for somewhere to eat. I heard "So Long, Marianne" coming from a cafe—'

Mum interrupts, 'That's the song about the Norwegian woman!'

She's obviously been listening very carefully to all the Leonard Cohen stories in the news. She hums a bit of the tune. I wait until she finishes. 'Go on,' she says.

'I loved the song but didn't know the singer,' I say, 'and my friend said—'

'It was Leonard Cohen – he's Canadian!'

'Yep,' I say.

'Was that before or after you became sick?' she asks.

'Before,' I say.

'You were very sick,' she says.

'I was,' I say, 'and my Canadian friend looked after me. He lent me some cassettes to listen to – Leonard Cohen and Gordon Lightfoot.'

But Mum's not interested in Gordon Lightfoot.

She has always had a very retentive memory, and once she takes an interest in a particular subject she quickly becomes an expert of sorts. Many years ago, Mum watched so many wildlife documentaries about sea creatures she said that she could easily be a midwife to a walrus. We all thought this was hilarious, but there was probably some truth in it.

The current special subject is Leonard Cohen. She knows about his time on Hydra with George Johnston and Charmian Clift, his various relationships, the names of his children and grandchildren.

'Do you know who Rufus Wainwright is?' she asks.

'Yes,' I say.

'Did you know that he has a daughter?'

'I think I read that somewhere.'

'Her name is Viva, and Leonard Cohen's daughter, Lorca, is the mother.'

'Oh yeah,' I say. 'I remember reading that.'

'Rufus,' says Mum, and the way she says his name makes it sounds like she knows him personally, 'is married to a man called …' She falters. 'Look up Rufus's husband's name on the Google,' she says.

I am forever the obedient daughter, and look up Rufus Wainwright. 'Jörn Weisbrodt,' I say.

'Yes, that's right, Jörn', says Mum. 'How do you spell that?'

'J, O with an umlaut, R, N,' I say.

'Must be German. Is he German?'

I've shut my laptop, so I open it again and confirm that Jörn is in fact German, but he lives in Toronto with Rufus. I shut my laptop again.

I am a bit blown away by how much time Mum must have spent over this past week just sitting in her chair, listening to the radio. As usual, I feel slightly guilty about the fact that I haven't done more with her.

But she seems positively chipper with her new knowledge of Leonard. She tells me that only days ago he released his most recent, and now last, album.

She tells me, with incredulity in her voice, 'He was eighty-two!'

I can't work out if she means that eighty-two is too young to die or if she's amazed that someone of eighty-two was still touring and making work. When I ask her, she says, 'Both!'

'Do you know the song "Dance Me to the End of Love"?' she asks.

'I love that song,' I say.

Mum hums a couple of bars. She has it down pat.

'Impressive!' I say when she stops.

'Not really,' she says. 'I've heard it so much over the past week that there would be something seriously wrong with me if I couldn't retain the tune.'

She may not be walking properly, she may be having problems with her heart, but there sure is nothing wrong with her memory.

'It reminds me of Robert Frost's "Acquainted with the Night",' she says.

'Yes,' I agree, 'there is something similar about the notion of the journey's end.'

Mum nods. We sit for a moment in silence.

'Have you ever seen Leonard Cohen in concert?' she eventually asks.

'Yes,' I say. 'One of the best concerts I've ever been to. He was so charming and elegant. He had these backup singers called the Webb Sisters, who sang beautiful harmonies and did a cartwheel as part of their choreography!'

'A cartwheel!' Mum says. 'Were they wearing trousers?'

'I can't remember,' I say.

'They must have been,' she says.

I don't say anything. It amuses me that Mum finds this particular detail interesting.

'Can you do a cartwheel?' Mum asks.

'Nope.'

'Michael could do cartwheels,' she says.

'I know,' I say.

'And walk on his hands, and do headstands and handstands.'

I smile and nod. Mum has been talking quite a bit about Michael of late. She seems to have forgotten all the bad bits and only talks about the good things.

'Remember the time he and Julie drove the children across the Gunbarrel Highway?' she asks.

I nod. They were towing a trailer and the axle broke out in the middle of nowhere, and Michael and Julie managed to fix it by themselves. When they were good together, they were excellent. We are momentarily lost in our thoughts.

'Have you met Leonard?' Mum asks.

'No, Mum,' I laugh. 'Unfortunately Leonard couldn't fit in a rendezvous with little Becky Blister when he was last in the country!'

'That's a shame,' she says. 'He seemed like a nice man.'

I look at her and see no hint of a smile, and I realise she's being serious. We've been having a few conversations like this. They are almost on point, but also slightly off-kilter. To an outsider, they would just seem like quirky conversations, but they worry Tony and me. Mum is alert and engaged, but something else is happening, something I haven't seen before. I feel I need to ask her a few practical questions and see how she responds.

But when I look over at Mum in her huge vinyl recliner, I notice she's lying right back with her eyes closed. She's gently humming 'Dance Me to the End of Love', and I realise our conversation is over.

Tony

I'm on the bus back from a meeting in Camooweal, and my old boss from Melbourne rings. 'Are you submitting an application for the director of policy and development?' Austin asks. 'It closes tomorrow.'

I've been toying with the idea, as it would be a significant promotion from the job that's on hold for me until April. But I'm hesitating, as I know that even if my application is successful, I won't take the job if Diana is still alive. Diana has had some seriously bad days in recent weeks and it feels like she could go at any time, but then a day or two later she'll be completely fine and it feels like she'll live for another ten years.

At Austin's prompting, I do the maths. It'll take weeks for

a selection panel to be assembled, and another week or two to select a shortlist. It seems likely that by the time they start scheduling interviews, it'll be so close to Christmas that key people will be away and they'll have no choice but to put the whole thing off until the New Year. I quietly lodge an application.

I feel guilty, as if I'm betraying Beck and Diana, and potentially setting up another unnecessary decision crisis. But I don't want to take the risk that Diana will die while the recruitment process is afoot. I want it all. Two days later, the HR manager rings me to schedule an interview for the following week. 'Yeah, sure – that's great,' I lie.

I don't have too much time to think about it, as in ten days I have a large meeting planned, at which the decision on the gas pipeline will be made. The negotiating team, made up of senior representatives of the key families, believes we've negotiated a good deal, but there's an outstanding question as to how the financial compensation will be distributed. Some families feel they are entitled to a greater share than other families, as they believe they are the ones who speak for the country over which the pipeline will be laid. Others want it shared evenly between the families. Others think it should be used for community development. Some want it put into trust for scholarships for kids and medical emergencies. I've been harangued on an almost daily basis by some people, who keep giving me their bank account details and requesting their share be paid to them straightaway – this is even before the deal has been agreed to, let alone any money transferred.

Fortunately, the negotiating team agrees with me that we don't have time to sort out how the money will be distributed before the group has to decide whether to accept the deal or not, and that all we need to do for the time being is agree to put the money into a trust; a proper consultation process will occur in the new year to determine what to do with it. I know this is risky. It might take years to sort out the money.

Rebecca

I've barely slept. I quietly open the door to the bedroom where my brother Paul is sleeping, and peek in. He arrived a few days ago from Florida. He hasn't even bothered to get under the sheets – clearly he just hit the sack and stayed there all night. It's been stinking hot, he's got jet lag, and he only has a small fan in his room. Tony and I have the luxury of the splitty, but even with that we've not been sleeping very much. I close the door and let him sleep.

The night before, Tony, Paul and I all went to bed wondering if this was it. Would Mum be with us in the morning? She had not had a good twenty-four hours. In fact, this week has been very up and down. She's been bright enough and her conversation more or less on track, but she's seemed weak and slightly discombobulated.

Last night the plan was that she and Paul would come with Tony and me to a community Christmas carols event. Tony and I were singing with the community choir, and though I'm ambivalent about carols and feel like a hypocrite when singing them, I do like singing with our funny little choir. Mum loves carols and a community event, so a singalong under the stars seemed liked a good way to spend an evening. But I could sense hesitation from her about going, and there seemed to be an inordinate amount of discussion about logistics for what was really just a small outing.

Eventually, we all decided that Tony and I would go to the carols in Tony's work car, and Paul would take Mum in the Prius. Paul would bring the wheelie walker and Mum would use it to get into the showgrounds where the carols were being held. Our friends Majella and Shane had offered to get to the event early in order to grab a good spot for us so that Mum could be close to the gate and the stage. After the concert, Tony and I would go to dinner with Majella and Shane, while Paul and Mum would come home. Phew!

It's so good to have Paul here with us, both for his company and to share in what's happening with Mum. We've been waiting months for this visit. He had planned to come earlier in the year, but unexpectedly discovered he had heart problems and had to have triple bypass surgery. I had to keep this information from Mum for weeks, and it was a relief when the surgery was successful and he was out of the danger zone and I could tell her. Of course, Mum had worked out that something was wrong. She had heard snippets of my phone conversations with Paul and his wife, Belinda, and put two and two together. Now, months later, he is fighting fit and happy to be here.

One evening after dinner I suggested a drive to the lookout.

'Only if Mum comes too,' Paul said. Mum hesitated, and Paul added, 'We can stop at the roadhouse and get ice creams.'

'Goody!' said Mum. She was out of the chair almost before Paul had finished speaking.

Paul has brought a new pep and energy to the house. Not that we had been lacking in pep, so to speak, but having a fresh face here has definitely given us all a boost. Paul is generous by nature and interested in all sorts of things; in fact, his disposition is very similar to Mum's.

'It's so good to have you here,' I told him when we got to the lookout. We'd left Mum at the picnic table happily eating her ice cream. 'Mum's so pleased to have you around. You're like the prodigal son.'

'You and Tony have done all the hard work,' he said, 'and I just waltz in and get all the praise. Doesn't seem fair, does it?'

I caught his eye and we both laughed. I don't think about it like that. I'm just happy to have him around. There's an exercise that I sometimes do with participants when I'm running mental health groups. I ask, 'If you were in a situation and had to get rid of a body, who would you go to for help? Who would you ask who would be able to just get on with the task without judgement, discrimination or questions?' The exercise always leads to great discussions and laughter. Most people have one or two key people they could ask.

I would ask Paul. He would hate doing it – he hates anything illegal, hates any form of violence or abuse, and is a non-drinker, non-drug taker and general all-round good citizen – but he'd do it. He'd get on with the task and ask questions later. And the task at hand last night was getting Mum to the carols.

In the afternoon she had a shower and put a few rollers in her hair to prepare for the outing. I discussed with her what she was going to wear and if she needed anything ironed.

'I don't think I can go,' Mum announced just before it was time to leave.

'Why not?' I asked.

Mum couldn't answer, and I felt frustrated. We had spent so much time discussing this outing, and I knew my friends were getting there early to get a good spot for us. I just wanted to get us into the cars and on the road.

'Are you worried about using the wheelie walker?' I asked.

'No, it's not that. I just don't feel up for it.'

Paul tried. 'Don't you want to hear Rebecca and Tony sing? I'll help you with the wheelie walker and we'll park close to the gate.'

'I think an outing would be good for you,' I added unhelpfully.

But Mum was adamant: she was not going out. She went into the bedroom and then returned to the lounge in her nightie and brunch coat. She sat down in the recliner and we knew the discussion was over.

'I'll stay home,' Paul said, and Tony and I headed off alone.

The carols event was okay. It was nothing to rave about, but I knew Mum would have enjoyed it. By the time we got home, she'd gone to bed. Paul was worried about her and told us that she'd been unable to eat any dinner, and was unsettled and agitated. He took her pulse and it felt slow, then fast and then slow again. He wanted to take her to the hospital or call an ambulance, but she said she just needed to go to bed. Paul got her into bed but felt very uneasy.

I did what all parents do with a new baby: I stood beside her bed and watched to see her chest rise and fall to ensure she was breathing. I felt her forehead; she didn't seem hot, so I left her to sleep.

Paul, Tony and I sat outside on the verandah and discussed the fact that this could be it. We all knew that something was not right, so were prepared for the worst. Finally, we all went to bed.

I tossed and turned and found it hard to sleep, but at some stage must have drifted off. I woke this morning to the sound of Mum humming 'Dance Me to the End of Love'. Tony and I smiled, got up and got on with the day.

Tony

Paul has recruited me as his leading hand and we're doing some repairs on the house. We replace the wire in the screen doors and repair the dining table and chairs, but we don't have time to fix the verandah. After careful examination, Paul declares that I'm capable of doing it on my own after he leaves. I'm not at all convinced. I have no problem-solving skills when it comes to anything handy.

'Of course you do,' he says kindly.

'You don't truly know me,' I reply.

Not to be deterred, he develops a plan and escorts me to the hardware store to buy all the tools and timber I'll need. He then supervises me while I crouch, sweating, under the house and measure up the places for the screws and insert the supporting timber. After I fix one plank firmly in place, he announces that I'm good to fly solo. I'm astounded: for the first time in my life, I feel vaguely competent with a drill and saw. Now I have a plan for how I'll repair the verandah over the coming months.

I start on another section of the verandah while Beck, Paul and Diana get organised to run some errands in town. For some reason, Diana has been reluctant to use her wheelie walker, but Beck has packed it in the boot and is determined that Diana's going to use it this time.

'Bring back a pie and custard tart for my lunch, now that I'm a tradie,' I call out from under the verandah.

An hour later they return, errands completed. Paul helps Diana into the house, and Beck comes out the front to check on my progress. 'How did it go with the walker?' I ask.

'It stayed in the boot. Mum said she didn't feel like getting out of the car.'

I can tell Beck's exasperated, and is feeling worried about Diana's out-of-character belligerence.

'Did you go to the bakery?'

'Of course. As if Paul and Mum need any encouragement to do that.'

In the evening we head to the lake for a swim. Diana decides not to come and offers instead to start preparing dinner. Corned beef is on the menu, at Paul's request. We promise to be back in time to help with the trimmings. It's beautiful at the lake, and we linger longer than planned. We talk about the future. Paul urges us to do what's best for us, even if that means returning to Melbourne before Diana dies. 'I've spoken to Mum,' he says. 'She's agreed to go into the nursing home, if necessary.'

This is the first time Diana has ever made such a concession. Beck and I look at each other and I know what she's thinking.

'That's good to know, Paul,' she says. 'And thanks for asking, but we're here until the end.'

I nod in agreement.

Rebecca

Paul encourages me to find a contractor to do the restumping on the house, but I'm overwhelmed by the scale of the job. 'Can't you just organise it all?' I say.

'I can get you started, but you need to have the information to manage the project once I'm gone,' he says.

I feel like a sulky youngest child. I'm tired of making decisions. I want my brother to take over.

Paul draws up a map of the stumps under the house and works out how many need to be replaced and how many just need some repair. Together we make a list of companies and contractors that do restumping work. Again, I want Paul to make the phone calls, but he tells me I have to do it. I can't believe how pathetic I am with this. Paul sits with me while I make the calls.

'Yep?' answers the builder.

'Oh, hi,' I say. 'Is this Smith Contractors?'

'Yep,' says the builder.

'Oh, okay … good … right. My name is Rebecca and I'm looking for a builder to do some restumping at my house in Soldiers Hill.'

I wait for the builder to reply but he stays silent.

'So … yeah,' I continue, 'we're looking for the restumping to happen as soon as possible.'

Again, I wait; again, silence.

'Are you available?'

'Nope.'

This time I pause. 'Right,' I eventually say. 'Do you know a builder who might be able to do the work?'

'Nope.'

'Okay … well … thanks for your time.'

'Yep,' says the builder, and the phone call ends.

This phone call repeats a number of times; we take to calling it the 'yep, yep, nope, nope, yep' minimalist tradie convo. We can't understand why they don't want the work. A builder eventually tells us that no one will do restumping work in the summer. 'Too hot under them old houses,' he tells us.

Eventually, we compile a shortlist of contractors who will come and give us some quotes. Paul prints out the map he's done, plus all the other information the tradies will need. I am grateful for this and finally feel I have enough information to manage the project.

Mum sits in her chair and listens to some of our conversations, but also spends a fair amount of time nodding off. She's in good spirits but by night-time she fades again. She is overly hot and listless. I get her into bed and sponge her down and try to make her as comfortable as possible. I ask her to describe what she's feeling but she can't. I stay with her until she dozes off.

Paul, Tony and I sit on the verandah and have the same conversation as the previous night, and wonder what the new day will bring.

Tony

A pattern is starting to emerge. Beck is worried. She makes sure that we don't have dinner too late, and is vigilant about keeping up Mum's drinks and snacks through the day.

Today, when I get home, Diana has her hair in rollers. 'She's putting an effort in tonight,' Beck says.

'That's a good sign, isn't it?' Paul replies.

'She knows there are going to be photos,' Beck retorts.

Tonight we're going for dinner at the Barkly Hotel. It's Paul's farewell dinner, and all the Mount Isa family will be there.

'Are we taking the wheelie walker out for another drive?' I ask.

'Sure, why not?' says Beck. 'You never know, tonight might be our lucky night.'

As we walk into the hotel, we see Aunty Doris King and her daughter Jackie, who I know through work. Then, inside, we run into Beck's social work student Lynette and her husband, Clayton, who come over to our table for a chat.

We talk about their work Christmas function and the dress-up theme of 'Come as your favourite star'.

Diana pipes up: 'I know who Tony could go as!'

We all laugh. Over the years I've frequently been mistaken for my brother Paul. As we get older, the resemblance gets stronger. This is the same for all my brothers. Beck and my sister-in-law Linda have a long-running joke that when all the Kelly men retire, we could form a cover band and travel the world singing Paul Kelly songs and doing impersonations.

Diana then blurts out: 'Elvis! Tony could go as Elvis!'

Everybody laughs even more, and Diana is very pleased with herself. I feel slightly embarrassed. I don't look at all like Elvis, nor do I have any of his moves. I glance across at Beck, who raises her eyebrows and frowns.

Regardless, it's a great night. We take photos and Diana glows. Back at home we remove the again unused wheelie walker from the boot. No one says a word. After Diana goes to bed, Paul, Beck and I retire to the verandah.

'That was a good night,' Paul says.

'Yeah, but what about the Elvis comment?' Beck says. 'Got any moves for us, Big T?'

We discuss the night and Diana some more. It feels like we're in some kind of holding pattern: we know something is going on but we don't know what.

Rebecca

Today is Wednesday and I have to go to work at Headspace. Paul is looking after Mum and taking her to a medical appointment. Mum has been fitted with a monitor in order to measure her heart rate so the doctors can determine what's happening and adjust her medication if needed. We're all hopeful, but also pragmatic. For someone who's ninety-two years of age, how much difference can medication really make? At what point does intervention seem futile?

Tonight I'm going to Jorja's primary school graduation dinner, and Tony picks me up after work. 'Diana's back in hospital,' he says when I get in the car.

At the appointment there was alarm from one of the staff about her heart rate. It transpired that she needed to be back in hospital. I can't help but feel a certain relief. We all know that something's been up, so hospital seems like the logical place for Mum to be right now.

Paul stays at the hospital with Mum, and Tony drives me to the dinner. He'll then head home and collect Mum's things and go back to the hospital and wait with Paul. This is hard for me as, to date, I've done all the medical appointments and hospital visits, but I know I need to go to the dinner for Jorja.

There are tears at the graduation dinner. The family tradition for the grandchildren and great-grandchildren is to have their photograph taken with Mum underneath the frangipani trees on the day of their graduation. Tonight Jorja has missed out. She is very close to Mum – or GG, as she calls her – and she's very disappointed. 'Madlyn and Ashley have grad photos with GG but not me!' she cries.

'I know,' I say, and wrap my arms around her.

'I knew this would happen,' she says.

'She didn't mean it to happen,' I say.

'I know,' says Jorja, 'but it just feels unfair.'

I don't say anything. I just keep my arms around her.

'Will she be in hospital for long?' Jorja asks.

'I hope not!' I say, keeping my tone upbeat.

Later that night, Paul, Tony and I all meet back at the house. It has taken quite some time for Mum to settle at the hospital but now she's asleep. We do our regular evening stint on the verandah. Tomorrow Paul has to fly back to the States. He says that if Mum dies over the next few weeks he won't be able to come back. He's working on a project in Mexico and needs to get back to work. We understand.

I can't stay in the room as Paul says goodbye to Mum. I just can't bear to watch. They both know this is it – the moment when a mother and her child say goodbye forever. I can't imagine having to do that with my own children. Many of us never get a chance to say goodbye to the ones we love, though. I leave them alone and let them have their final moments together.

I take Paul to the airport and say goodbye. We'll see him again in a year or two.

I go back to the hospital. Mum is not good. She's very agitated. She seems to be having trouble breathing, and is very uncomfortable. I tell the doctor.

'Is everything organised with your mum's advance health directive?' she asks.

'Everything is filled out and signed by Mum and her doctor,' I say. 'I just need to get a justice of the peace to sign it.'

'You should get that organised as soon as possible,' she tells me.

'What's happening?' I ask. 'Is something wrong?'

'It's procedure,' the doctor says. 'Just procedure.'

But I suspect it is something more.

I try a few different numbers to find a JP but don't have any luck. I ring Florence, the business manager at Headspace. I tell her what's happening and she says she'll try to find a JP for me. I am grateful to have someone else on the job.

One of the nurses at the hospital tells me she thinks one of the reception staff might be a JP. I go down and enquire, but they tell me this isn't the case. Then one of the staff remembers that there is someone in finance who is a JP. She rings that person and I speak to her. She comes up to the ward at lunchtime and signs the papers.

I spend the rest of the afternoon at the hospital. Belinda and her girls join me after school, and we try to get Mum engaged in a crossword but she can't focus. Tony arrives in the early evening, and together we try to get Mum comfortable. She finally settles, and the nurses tell me it's best that we leave so Mum can get some sleep.

Tony

Beck and I come home from the hospital late and go straight to bed, but the house feels strangely quiet and empty with Paul gone and Diana in hospital and it takes ages for either of us to go to sleep. The next morning I head into work for a final planning session ahead of next week's pipeline meeting.

An hour later, Beck rings to tell me Diana has had a massive stroke and is in a coma. I make my excuses from the meeting and go straight to the hospital. By the time I arrive, Diana has been moved from the noisy ICU into a quieter room upstairs. We are told there is no coming back for Diana. A blood clot has lodged in her brain and she's lost a lot of brain function. Another clot has lodged in her leg, causing thrombosis. Diana waves one arm in the air and groans. Beck gently takes hold of her arm, places it on the bed and strokes it. 'It's okay, Mum,' she tells her. 'I'm here. Belinda too. Tony's just arrived from work. I'm sure he's got a crossword. Everything's okay.'

I touch the leg with the clot; it is deeply cold. I remember the day after my dad died. I was seven years old, and when I got home from school he was laid out in his coffin in the study. I touched his forehead; it was cold. Diana's leg feels the same. The cold of death.

Beck looks at me. Grief crosses her face but she is calm. We hold each other's gaze and nod. Beck smiles a closed-mouth smile. I smile back. We know we've got this.

Rebecca

For the next four days, Tony, Belinda and I stay by Mum's side and gently care for her. We brush her hair, clean her mouth, massage her limbs, paint her nails, read to her, sing to her, do crosswords and laugh and cry.

In the evening we turn down the lights, take sips of whisky from Tony's hip flask, and play all our and Mum's favourite songs. We play *Death's Dateless Night*, the latest album by Tony's brother Paul. It is perfect for the occasion.

During the day, friends come to the hospital to pay their respects, and there are lots of phone calls and messages. Belinda calls her siblings and they speak to their grandma. We don't know if she can hear them, but that's irrelevant. Samantha is on holidays in Hawaii and is desperate to get back, but it's not possible to change or rearrange her flights. I can hear the pain in her voice when I speak to her. The only consolation is that she's in Hawaii, which Mum has always said is her favourite place in the world.

In the midst of all this, I receive a call from my cousin Paddi to tell me that her mother, my aunty Eileen, has just died. Eileen was Dad's sister, and the last of Dad's siblings to go. She was ninety-eight, and we all thought she would live on to get her 'telegram from the Queen'. When Mum first married Dad, they lived with Eileen and her husband, Henry, in their house in Mount Isa until they found a place of their own. For over fifty years they lived one street from each other.

I tell Paddi that I'm in the hospital and waiting for Mum to die. It seems fitting that these two should die within days of each other. They've been friends for over seventy years, and up until now still connected with weekly phone conversations.

I ask the nurses how long this is likely to go on for. They all say the same thing: 'Everyone is different. She'll go when she's ready.' We suspect she's waiting for something, or someone.

Sunday night is the longest night. Mum wheezes and rattles, and although she's unconscious she seems uncomfortable. I don't sleep. I hold her hand and say many times, 'It's okay, Mum, you can go.'

At 4 am I leave the room for a short time and go outside. I need some air. I wander up and down in front of the hospital. One of the security staff comes over to me and starts talking. 'What department do you work in?' he asks.

'I don't work here,' I say.

'But I see you here every day,' he says.

'I'm with my mum,' I tell him. 'We're waiting for her to die.'

The security man nods and touches my shoulder. I say nothing.

In the morning, Tony goes to the airport to pick up David, who is flying in from Mackay. A little after 9 am, David walks into the hospital room, holds Mum's hand and says, 'Mum, it's me, Dave.' He sits down beside her and says, 'I love you, Mum.'

I start gathering my things. The plan is to let David have some time with Mum by himself, and for me to go home and have a shower.

'Beck,' says Tony.

I turn around. 'Yeah?'

'I think she's going,' he says.

Mum breathes in noisily, then out, and then she stops.

We hold her hands and say nothing. We look at each other, and through tears smile gently.

'She waited for you,' I say to David eventually.

'Yeah,' says David. 'I thought she would.'

I've heard stories like this over the years but have always taken them with a grain of salt. Are people really able to choose when they die? Do people really wait for certain family members to arrive before they let go? Can people in their last breathing moments hear the voices of loved ones and know who is present and who is still missing? Well, today I say yes. Today I have witnessed it.

Tony

David and I head over to Belinda's for a swim. Beck has gone home, saying she'll come later. We sit in the pool with drinks in our hands, still somewhat stunned by what we have just witnessed. Seppo and the kids join us, and we swim and move gently around each other, talking quietly. We know over these past few days we have all been part of something beautiful, and we feel touched by grace and goodness.

Rebecca

The phone rings again and I contemplate not answering. It has rung nonstop since I came back from the hospital. The house is finally quiet. But of course I answer.

'Hello, Rebecca. It's your aunty Veronica.'

I pause. It takes a few moments for my brain to catch up with my ears. And then it kicks in and I don't know if I want to laugh, cry or scream. We have waited thirty-seven years for this phone call.

'Hello, Aunty Veronica.' Suddenly I am sixteen again.

'I just wanted to ring you to tell you how much I admired your mum. She was a great mother, wife and sister.'

There's so much I want to say. Where were you? Where were you when Michael died? Where were you when Dad died? Where were you when Mum needed you the most? But I don't say any of these things. I take a leaf out of Mum's book, let bygones be bygones and remain in the present.

'It's good to hear your voice,' I say.

'It's good to hear yours too,' she replies.

We talk a bit more and make plans to speak again after the funeral.

I hang up, and think about how I'd love to be able to tell Mum about that conversation.

Tony

'I've been in contact with the funeral home and the church and we're set for Friday,' Beck announces.

We're all here – the nieces and nephews, partners and children, David, Beck and me – gathered in the lounge room for the first of what I expect to be a number of meetings throughout the week.

'We'll need to organise an order of service, music, the wake,' she continues. 'Can anyone think of anything else?'

'Pallbearers,' adds David.

'Yes – who wants to be a pallbearer?' Becks asks.

'Not just the boys,' Madlyn chips in.

'When can we view Grandma?' Sam asks.

She and the rest of the Mount Isa family were very close to Diana, and their grief is profound. Beck has to tread carefully. I fear there may be a struggle for ownership of the grief. This is fed by a lingering worry that the others have felt usurped by Beck and me. Worry that we (actually, mainly me) might be seen as coming in and replacing the nieces and nephews in their relationship with their grandmother. Blow-ins from down south, just here for a couple of years, while they've been here always, a constant source of company and support. I know this isn't likely, but right now, with a funeral to organise, and grief coursing through each of us, everyone is under pressure. If things are not managed carefully, fissures could open over the next couple of days.

'I think we should play Dolly Parton's "Islands in the Stream" as the coffin leaves the church,' Brian announces.

Belinda agrees enthusiastically.

I look across at Beck, and from her face I can see that she doesn't agree. I feel anxious.

'That's a song for your funeral, not Mum's,' Beck teases Brian, who is a huge Dolly Parton fan. Everyone laughs and the tension breaks. Also, by saying *Mum*, not *Grandma* or *Diana*, Beck has subtly but clearly asserted her status. It is her mother we are burying, and ultimately she and David will call the shots.

We settle on Johnny Cash's 'Will the Circle Be Unbroken'.

The following day I have a phone interview for the job. The house in Madang Street is bulging at the seams, with family coming and going. The only private place I can find is our bedroom. I sit on the bed with the air conditioner on high and the venetians rattling.

The first question I'm asked is direct: 'Will you take the job if offered, given the need to look after your mother-in-law?'

'She died yesterday,' I tell the panel. They're shocked and offer to reschedule. 'No, I'm right to proceed,' I say.

At that point Beck and her seventeen-year-old nephew, James, commence a loud conversation outside the bedroom door.

'Do you wax your eyebrows?' Beck asks James.

'No, I get them threaded,' James replies in a low rumble.

'Do you?' Beck is clearly surprised.

'Yeah. Threading. It's really good.'

'I get mine waxed,' Beck babbles on.

'Excuse me,' I say to the panel, and get off the bed and open the door. 'I'm in the middle of an interview!'

Beck and James scamper down the hallway.

By the end of the day the job is mine.

Swimming later that evening with Beck and Georgina (who has just arrived in town for the funeral), we discuss whether I should take the job. 'I like it here,' I admit.

'You can't like it too much,' Beck retorts, 'given you've got yourself another job before we've even buried Mum!'

Georgina is aghast that I would even consider not taking the job. She makes no effort to hide her distaste for Mount Isa. 'You're coming back. That's the end of it.'

I duck under the water, push myself off the wall and glide over to the other side. 'You're right,' I tell her when I resurface.

David has a bit too much to drink and becomes argumentative on the way home from Belinda's. Later that night, Beck tells me how she's feeling. 'I'm pissed off with David,' she says. 'I need him sober and by my side.'

'Tell him exactly that,' I encourage her.

She does so the next morning. 'David, you're funny and charming,' she begins.

'When I'm not drinking, you mean?' he interrupts. He's in the kitchen cooking breakfast for everyone.

'Yes, when you're sober. The aunties and uncles have always liked you the most. It gives me the shits, actually. Anyway, we've got a big few days ahead and we need to do this together.'

David nods. 'Fair enough.'

'Can you be the driver for tonight's barbecue?' Beck asks. 'Pick people up from the airport, and ferry 'em to the lake and back to the hotel?'

'Sure, of course,' he says.

'That'd be great, thanks.'

Our friend Ruth and my brother Martin arrive, along with Diana's sister Mary and her daughter, Caroline. David shuttles everyone back and forth, charming them along the way. I see Beck start to relax.

At the end of the night, Michael calls out to David as he's bundling Aunty Mary into the car: 'Next time we have a barbie, Uncle Dave, you should join us.'

David just laughs.

Rebecca

The rain has made the church cool, and the funeral goes off without a hitch. Mum was always clear with me about what she wanted: flowers, colourful outfits and good music. If we insisted, we could show photos. 'But go easy on the wailing,' she'd say. The funeral is colourful and joyful and full of music, but not without some tears.

I'm touched that many of my work colleagues and friends from Headspace come to the funeral. Most of Mum's friends are long gone, but even so the church is full. Ash and Tara play her favourite hymns, and I swear I can hear her humming. The music is uplifting and true to Mum.

There are a lot of speeches and readings – me, Belinda, Samantha, Brian, Tony, Georgina, Madlyn, Ashley and Jorja. Initially I thought that might be too much, but it's perfect. We all need to speak, and our words are a combination of poignant, funny and deeply loving. The minister acknowledges Mum's long and devoted relationship with Christianity and with this church. I had worried that the service might seem a bit cloying, but my fears are unnecessary. The minister graciously takes the lead from us and pitches his words at the same level. It is fitting that Mum should be remembered with such admiration and dignity.

The burial also goes smoothly. The night before, Georgina and Ruth drove around town picking frangipani flowers from neighbourhood trees. We put them into plastic bags and popped them in the freezer. This morning we transferred them to an esky and then to baskets, and they've stayed perfectly in shape. Everyone takes a handful and throws the flowers into the grave. David speaks at the gravesite, and his words are gentle and moving.

After the funeral we go to the wake and drink 'pine ale', Mum's favourite mocktail, made from a combination of pineapple juice and ginger ale. We eat small sandwiches and little pastries. A few people have a beer or a wine but it's all very laid-back.

Throughout it all, I keep thinking: Mum would have loved this!

Tony

The day after the funeral, I attend the pipeline authorisation meeting. Over a hundred people are there. Many have come from the coast or from the across the border in the Northern Territory.

The pipeline company executives make their pitch and leave. I advise on the deal we have negotiated. Representatives from the key families give their opinions, and the deal is debated back and forth. It doesn't seem that many people have any problems with the deal, but the agreement nearly comes unstuck when we turn to how the financial component will be distributed. Finally, everyone consents to place the funds in trust and allow for a full consultation process in the new year. The anxious pipeline execs are invited back in and the agreement is signed.

I'm buoyed by the success of the meeting, and by the emotion of the past week. Aunty Doris, one of the senior elders, comes up to thank me. She remembers Diana from the Barkly Hotel the week before. She takes my arm and tells me what a lovely woman my mother-in-law was.

'Rebecca's your wife?' she continues. I nod yes. 'What beautiful blue eyes she has.'

I agree.

'Give her my condolences.'

'I will.'

'Where is she?'

'Home with the family.'

'That's where you need to be.' Doris dismisses me with a wave of her hand.

Rebecca

By Saturday lunchtime, most people have headed back out of town. My nephew James decides to stay on in Mount Isa for a few days with us. I am really pleased.

In the late afternoon all the nieces and nephews come over and we have drinks and snacks under the frangipani trees. I still can't quite believe that Mum isn't with us, and keep popping my head into her bedroom to check if she's there or not.

I feel as though I have barely slept for over a week, and that – combined with a tad too much wine – results in me toppling off my chair and into the garden bed below the trees. I scream as I go down.

'Oh my god!' screams Belinda, but hers is not a scream of fright but of hilarity. 'Aunty,' she says, 'what are you doing down there?'

'Help me up!' I cry.

'Your dress!' says Samantha. 'Your dress!'

I look down and can see that my dress has come right up and is showing my underpants.

The nieces and nephews are in hysterics.

'Aunty's lost it!' says Michael.

'Taxi!' calls Brian.

Eventually, two of them pull me up out of the garden bed and plonk me back on my chair. It is the comical moment we've all been looking for. The new family matriarch has had her debut moment in the garden bed!

Tony comes home from his meeting and joins us in the yard until eventually the others leave.

We sit on the verandah and have a much-needed cup of tea. We are both so tired, but everything feels calm.

Tony and I decide that he will take the new job back in Melbourne. I'll stay in Mount Isa and manage the restumping of the house and finish my other jobs. I'll also sort through the contents of the house, and then we'll put it on the market. We suspect all this might take four to six months. Also, I've recently accepted a new contract at the Mount Isa campus of James Cook University, and I still have work at Headspace. It all feels very doable.

Tony goes inside and puts on some music. When he comes back out, we raise our cups to Mum and the past two years.

We have done it. We have given to Mum what she had spent her entire lifetime giving to others.

The next song comes on. It is Leonard Cohen, 'Dance Me to the End of Love'. Tony and I hold hands, go inside and dance.

EPILOGUE

Tony

The first ten metres are the hardest, swimming through the duckweed to get to the open water beyond. It's midway through summer and the duckweed is rampant; even the canoeists have been unable to stay on top of it. With its long tentacles reaching towards the sun from the murky depths, the weed tickles my belly as I skim over the top.

This is my last swim in the lake before I head south. Diana's been dead for over a month, and in a couple of weeks I'll be taking up the new job in Melbourne. Since the funeral and Christmas, Beck and I have settled into an easy and peaceful routine. We realise it's the first time we've lived with just each other for twenty-four years. We're revelling in it. Diana's mark is still all through the house, but over the two years we have shaped it to our liking and it feels very comfortable.

I'm back at work but the pace is gentle, in keeping with the time of year. I plod away at fixing the verandah on the weekends and evenings. We discover the neighbours are away, and sneak into their pool for the occasional skinny-dip. The rain comes, and we drive down to the causeway and watch the flooding river flow over the road. We plant a mango in the front yard in memory of Diana, knowing we won't be here to see it grow.

Beck isn't returning to Melbourne with me immediately, as she has work commitments to honour and the house to prepare for sale. Also, I suspect Beck wants more time to say goodbye. I know she's really torn about leaving. Rationally, she knows that leaving's the only real option, but emotionally she's not ready. I worry she never will be. The west is where Beck is from, and I've come to realise it's where she's the happiest. I worry that a return to Melbourne will lead to a slow but steady dampening of her spirits.

Today there are storms circling the lake and the water is quite rough. My legs drag and I stray off course. The line of yellow buoys that delineates the swimming area from the speedboats and jet skis isn't getting any closer, and it feels like a slog. The childhood warning not to be in the water in an electrical storm rings in my ears as I scan the horizon. Eventually I find my rhythm and my mind starts to drift.

The last time I was out here, Diana came with us. She sat at one of the picnic tables and enjoyed the softening ambience as the hot afternoon came to a close. Who would have guessed that nine days later she would be dead?

I startle as a scratchy strand of duckweed wraps itself around my neck. My flow broken, I take a mouthful of water. It's then I think of the mine upstream and all the pollutants in the run-off pouring into the dam with the wet. I try to reassure myself that heavy metals sink and would be safely lodged in the sludge at the bottom of the lake. David's taunt that people release salties into the lake unsettles me even more. I pause, lift up my goggles and scan the lake. Pointless, I know; it's the ones you don't see that get you.

We fire up the barbecue after our swim and watch as the

surrounding hills and rocks go from yellow to orange to red. There's lightning in the distance, and the rumble of thunder rolls back across the lake.

Despite the sadness of Diana's death, I am not bereft. Rather, I feel deeply enriched by the experience of the last two years, and I have no doubt I'll miss this hard town, nestled against the mine. I'll miss the heat and the house shaking from the twice-daily blasts deep underground. I'll miss the road trains changing gears out on the highway, and the sound of air conditioners rattling through the night. I'll miss the intimacy and the space and the focus that isolation provides.

I feel grateful to have had the opportunity to live with Diana and help her see out her life with grace and laughter. I feel deep love for Beck, who brought me to her town and who flourished under the open sky. I have a rich life, and a family I love, awaiting me in Melbourne.

Rebecca

I shed tears as the plane lifts off the runway and into the sky; they're tears of sadness, relief and pride. Today is 5 December 2017. It is exactly one year since Mum died, and I'm leaving Mount Isa for good.

It's a bittersweet moment. While on one hand it's a relief to finally have the house sold, it filled me with a deep sadness to close the door at Madang Street for the last time.

I won't hear the sounds of the doorknobs, light switches or the confounded rattling venetian blinds ever again.

I won't spend early mornings in my soccer shorts and singlet, watering the garden and watching the lorikeets as they feast on the flowering grevillea.

I won't sit on the front verandah and while away the evening.

I won't stand on the back ramp and watch storms roll in from the gulf.

I won't sit under the house and marvel at how lucky I am to have a fella who thinks that this carved-out bunker is paradise.

I won't drive up Madang Street and at the last moment swerve to avoid Maleka.

But a new excitement awaits me. I will, finally, go back to my family and life in Melbourne. I'm looking forward to living with Tony again. We've rented a groovy-looking pad in Northcote, so maybe we'll finally get to have those post-work drinks at a Spanish or Japanese bar.

Tony has spent the last twelve months living and working in Melbourne, and while we've had great long weekends over that time, it's not the same as living together.

He came up a little while ago to help with the final farewell. Last weekend we opened the house and yard up for a huge garage sale. It took days to set it all up, and then further days to shift all the things we didn't sell. I made my first foray into online selling, and sold all of Michael's work tools, each engraved with his name. They had been in the shed for twenty-three years, avoided or ignored: too many, too hard, too sad.

The house was finally restumped. Tony, David, Belinda, Samantha and I ripped up carpet, sanded floors, and painted the entire house so it was ready for a sale. I engaged an excellent real estate agent, who immediately understood exactly what we wanted to do with the house and showcased it as a retro beauty. Mum and Dad would have been amazed, and so proud. After just six weeks on the market, we sold. I did the final negotiations from my car in Darwin, amid a raging storm.

Over these twelve months I've finished my contract at Headspace, worked as the social work clinical lead for the Mount

Isa branch of James Cook University, written my first screenplay, worked on the inaugural Mount Isa Youth Short Film Festival and finished a new play that will have a season in Melbourne next year. I've been busy, but in between the business I have felt Mum's absence acutely.

In the weeks after Mum's death, I spent hours replying to the many sympathy cards the family received. As 25 December got closer, the Christmas cards also started rolling in. I replied to each one, relaying the news of Mum's death. This produced another series of sympathy cards and I replied to those too. When I mentioned this to my friends, they told me to leave it and do it in the new year. But I knew that was not an option. Sitting at the kitchen table each evening, I felt as though I was channelling Mum. Slowly and steadily I worked through the pile.

Just before Christmas, I harvested my first pineapple. Samantha and I made a video of the act and posted it online. It felt good to do something funny. I knew that Mum would have loved the interest it created.

Yesterday afternoon Samantha and I went to the cemetery so I could say goodbye to Mum, Dad, Michael and Grandma. I lay on the grass beside Mum's and Dad's graves and told them stories about the last twelve months. Some stories were happy: Samantha and Thomas's wedding, the Easter weekend when the whole family got stuck into painting the house, the pots of healthy plants that I sold and gave away. Some stories were sad: Belinda and Seppo have moved away from town, and their marriage has ended.

Our family now has more people 'living' in the cemetery than in town. After almost seventy years, Samantha and Thomas are the last family members left in the Isa, and they too will soon be gone.

When Sam and I got home from the cemetery, we saw Tony having beers on the front lawn with Shawn and Cheyenne. After much angst, Tony had decided to give them our swags. They would be too expensive to ship to Melbourne, and it's unlikely they'll get much use from now on.

'Wow. You sure?' said Shawn. He was really pleased.

'Yeah. We'd be honoured. We've really liked getting to know you,' said Tony.

He's right, we have enjoyed knowing Shawn and Cheyenne and the kids (perhaps not their animals as much), and wish them well.

Last night I went around the house and left a small plastic pineapple in a corner of every room – one last job for the Pineapple Princess. Mum would have thought it horribly kitsch, but it would have made her laugh all the same. This morning Tony and I helped the removalists get the last items onto the truck, and after a few final photographs we closed the front door for the last time.

I look through the plane window at the red earth and sparse vegetation. Though it offers very little relief, I know I'll miss this too. These colours are part of me and I wonder how I'll go without them, and without the endless sunlight and vitamin D.

I rest my head against Tony's shoulder. I'm exhausted. It's been a huge week.

Never in my wildest dreams did I think that I would feel such a tremendous tug about the decision to leave. Some days I would call Tony and say, 'I want to stay, just one more year after this one, and then I'll come back!' I knew, however, that one more year would probably lead to ten more, which would eventually lead to me being the fifth family member in the cemetery.

If someone had told me three years ago that I'd feel like this, I would have told them they were mad. When we moved back here I had a task to do, and I was determined to do it as well as I could. I come from a long line of pragmatists, and when a job needs to be done, you just get on and do it. And then you leave.

Though at times over these past twelve months I have been

horribly lonely, I also felt the same love for the place that I had as a kid. It just felt so good to be home.

I'll miss so many things about this lifestyle, but most of all I'll miss being still so close to Mum. Over these last twelve months, I have spent many an hour sitting in her big green recliner in the lounge. Sometimes I would do a crossword puzzle or listen to the radio, but mainly I'd just turn off the splitty, open the front door and sit. After weeks of trying to sell the chair, I finally gave it my Turkish friend Ozzie for her art studio. Ozzie did not get to meet Mum, but I know they would have connected. Now the recliner has a happy new home.

I also spent many afternoons lying on Mum's bed in her room. Again, I wouldn't do anything, I'd just lie and think. Sometimes I'd open the door to Mum's wardrobe and smell her clothes. Eventually, I had to sort them all out. I distributed some things to the family and gave the rest to the charity shops. While I was doing it, I could almost hear Mum's voice: 'It's a thankless task but someone has to do it.'

Sometimes I would open her jewellery boxes and look at her things, but mainly I'd just lie on the bed, listen to the birds and think about Mum. I would think about how content she was in her last few years. Mum got what she wanted and what she deserved. She wanted to stay in the house and she deserved to be happy and safe, and we all played a part in making that happen.

Sometimes, when I'd lie on her bed, I would hear humming – a tuneless warble – and I couldn't help but join in.

I look through the window of the plane and can see the twinkling lights of Melbourne. I put my tray table up, dry my eyes, put on a bit of lippy and fluff up my hair. Just like Mum would have done.

I take Tony's hand and smile. I feel excited. I'm coming home to a new house, and to friends and family. A whole new chapter awaits us.

Diana Lister
8 February 1924 – 5 December 2016

ACKNOWLEDGEMENTS

We'd like to acknowledge that earlier versions of some parts of this book were first published in *The Big Issue* and the *Australian Indigenous Law Review*.

We want to thank Rebecca's family. Firstly, to her nieces and nephews Belinda, Brian, Michael and Samantha and their partners, and the great-nieces Madlyn, Ashley and Jorja, thank you for the continuous love and support you gave Diana. You brought her great joy. And to her brothers Paul and David and their families, who from afar gave us great encouragement: Diana loved you deeply.

Tony's family was always only a phone call, email or plane trip away. Some of you even made it up to visit. Thank you for your unconditional love.

There are of course our daughters, Georgina and Lucille, whose unselfishness and understanding gave us the freedom to do what we felt we needed to do. Thank you for keeping us current and don't worry – your turn will come.

Thank you to Diana's crew at St James the Great Anglican Church, Legacy Mount Isa, and the staff from the community health centre bus. Special thanks to Beryl, Susan, Betty, Marj,

Marlene, Barbara, Val, Ash, Sara and Heather. You made Diana's life rich and rewarding.

Then there is the legion of friends – new ones in Mount Isa who made us welcome and old ones from all over the country who were never far from our thoughts and who sent us messages, lent us their ear and on many occasions gave us meals and beds and made sure we never doubted this was the right thing to do.

All of you made it possible.

For this book, we'd like to thank everyone at UQP for taking a punt on two relatively unknown writers on this not-so-straight-forward two-handed project. Special thanks to Alexandra Payne for her initial belief and to Madonna Duffy, Cathy Vallance and Julian Welch for their deft guidance and ongoing encouragement.

We also want to thank each other for the willingness to give it a go and especially for the love.